LEARNING UNLEASHED

LEARNING UNLEASHED

Reimagining and Repurposing Our Schools

Evonne E. Rogers

ROWMAN & LITTLEFIELD
Lanham • Boulder • New York • London

Published by Rowman & Littlefield
A wholly owned subsidiary of The Rowman & Littlefield Publishing Group,
Inc.
4501 Forbes Boulevard, Suite 200, Lanham, Maryland 20706
www.rowman.com

Unit A, Whitacre Mews, 26-34 Stannary Street, London SE11 4AB

British Library Cataloguing in Publication Information Available

Library of Congress Cataloging-in-Publication Data

Names: Rogers, Evonne E., 1953- author.
Title: Learning unleashed : re-imagining and re-purposing our schools / Evonne E. Rogers.
Description: Lanham, Maryland : Rowman & Littlefield, 2016. | Includes bibliographical refer-
    ences and index.
Identifiers: LCCN 2016016240 (print) | LCCN 2016030727 (ebook) | ISBN 9781475829198
    (cloth : alk. paper) | ISBN 9781475829204 (pbk. : alk. paper) | ISBN 9781475829211 (Elec-
    tronic)
Subjects: LCSH: School improvement programs--United States. | Education--Aims and objectives-
    -United States. | Active learning--United States.
Classification: LCC LB2822.82 .R638 2016 (print) | LCC LB2822.82 (ebook) | DDC 371.2/07--
    dc23
LC record available at https://lccn.loc.gov/2016016240

∞ ™ The paper used in this publication meets the minimum requirements of
American National Standard for Information Sciences—Permanence of Paper
for Printed Library Materials, ANSI/NISO Z39.48-1992.

Printed in the United States of America

For Mom and Dad
Thank you for teaching me just about everything
I needed to know.

CONTENTS

PREFACE

WHY THIS BOOK?

What makes this book different from others that have tackled the question of what's wrong with our schools? For me, it's an entry point of sorts to the many questions, hunches, and revelations that have been swirling around in my mind for over fifty years. Given that I have spent my entire life in and around schools and believe passionately that learning is the most exciting and rewarding human endeavor, I decided to share what I have experienced and observed related to this industrial-aged experiment we call *school*.

Schools have not kept up with the changing world in which we live, nor have they provided peak learning experiences for most children. On the contrary, schools continue to experiment with recycled strategies and so-called research-based reforms that have little to no impact on student learning. What we see are isolated practices that may bring about small change but nothing substantial or long lasting.

Books are written touting the effects of these "proven" strategies, and the writers take their research on the road with an exorbitant price tag to match their claims. Educators flock to the conferences seeking the latest research that might make a difference for students. We then consume these strategies in massive quantities hoping to see results or find the silver bullet that will yank our students up to an acceptable level of performance.

We indoctrinate the teaching ranks on these highly effective, research-based strategies and hope for the kind of transfer that will equate to fewer dropouts and better test scores. However, what is happening on a regular basis in most schools and what we do quite well is force-fed learning. This is replicated every day all over the country and packaged as a "must-have" product called *school*.

Young people are spoon-fed random bits of information, told they must consume it within a certain time frame, and then ordered to regurgitate it on demand via a test. We are conditioning them to do this from the moment they arrive in our kindergarten classrooms until the time they leave, whenever that may be. The plan is to see them salivate at the very sight and sound of our voices so that they will want to consume whatever we are serving.

This may seem a rather unsavory description but consider this: Most young children come to school eager and excited to continue their quest for learning—you can see it in their faces. In order to manage the large numbers in our classrooms, we then proceed to "teach" the rules. These rules are stated, rehearsed, and revisited as needed. Staying in assigned seats, not talking, and doing your work are foundational to a productive classroom.

Once rules are established, we begin to teach subjects such as math, reading, science, and social studies. These subjects are presented as separate disciplines having their own merit, with a heavy textbook and loads of worksheets to prove it. Each subject has a set of discrete skills and concepts that one must master.

As time passes, these subjects appear to increase in difficulty and may or may not be well articulated from one year to the next. Obviously that doesn't matter. The goal is to consume all of it in rapid succession and prove retention on a test, usually with paper and pencil, which results in a grade.

The grades are ordered in priority status, with an A being the most coveted for those who regurgitate in an excellent manner. For some, this force-fed learning works well, or at least it appears that way by the test results. However, many teachers will tell you that after a summer break they spend way too much time reviewing what they expected their students to learn in the previous year. Others may observe some retention at test time, but frequently not much transfers moving forward.

What happens when the identified amount of information is not consumed rapidly enough in the allotted time frame or when the chunks of information get lodged or stuck and digestion is hampered? The most notable remedy is to repeat the process until it can be regurgitated effectively. Another strategy some employ is the push-through and catch-up method, which frequently results in severe indigestion and nausea. Those who open wide, ingest well, and develop a strong regurgitation response do well. Others, not so much.

And in the end, what has been accomplished? We have demonstrated our ability to "train" children to repeat facts and formulas without a shred of evidence that they really have understood or can transfer ideas and concepts to new or unique problems. This is played out when many of our students cannot apply what they've learned in new situations. It is also realized when students find themselves assigned to remedial courses in high school or college.

Some students are able to catch on quickly to the verbal scattering of information only to find themselves less and less engaged due to sheer boredom. These are often the students who abhor worksheets, detest the mounds of math problems assigned as homework, and have little patience for those who are slowing them down. They are categorized as bright or gifted. Schools tell us that they are supposed to have a different kind of curriculum according to their needs.

The school's response to the needs of these students is to differentiate the base curriculum until such a time that they can be channeled into Advanced Placement courses in high school. Some schools and districts offer a separate program for these children; others don't. Typically, the school's zip code or neighborhood often dictates the kind of programs that are offered to students who appear to learn more quickly.

A plea for more schooling and higher academic standards is the cry we hear across our nation. Some have indicated that if we start schooling at the tender age of three or four, little ones have an advantage later in life. Even with years of programs like Head Start or state preschools, we are told that our students are not entering college ready for the coursework and not entering the workforce fully prepared to meet the critical requirements of today's job market.

Some assert that continued funding for these early years programs will certainly provide a level playing field for all children. Many believe that stronger accountability and more rigorous standards will improve this situation. Others demand a total shift in the status quo with a growing groundswell of support for online education, homeschooling, and even un-schooling.

The most recent movement to improve schooling for all children emphasizes college and career readiness as many states adopted what is known as the rigorous "common core" standards. This movement is seen by some as the best effort yet to standardize what our children learn across the country. The logic behind this movement says if all children in the United States learn the same rigorous standards then all children will have a better chance for college and career.

To some, these standards are seen as an attempt to eradicate embarrassing inequities that still persist, especially in our large urban area school systems. Any such efforts are always under scrutiny and rightly so. When we attempt to create a common playing field, we automatically marginalize and disenfranchise large portions of the school population by virtue of their individuality and differences. We miss the point totally. Common does not equate to equal opportunity. I will talk about this later in the book.

We use high-stakes testing results to determine whether what we have taught has been learned. Over the years, we have used these results to identify any gaps in various student populations. These gaps are then analyzed more closely in order to see exactly which students are not performing well. The results are made public and scrutinized carefully by school boards and some parents. When the gaps are then acknowledged, it is the job of the schools to effectively address those gaps.

This is where the schooling system drops the ball and rarely retrieves it. Desperately attempting to close the gap, schools proceed to initiate interventions to raise the scores. There are very different approaches to tackling this problem, and exactly how it is done varies from school to school. Some employ instructional assistants to work on the basics with these identified students. Others provide a double dose of the same, hoping that more exposure to the material will work. Still others use costly remediation programs, often via computer, that drag students through varying levels of practice and difficulty.

We delude ourselves if we really believe that we have closed the achievement gap. The gap still exists. Where it's been reported to have narrowed leaves us wondering if the process of consume and regurgitate was mastered well enough to pass the test. No one knows for sure if there was retention or true learning.

There are two main problems that exist in this persistent gap. One problem is that we have assisted in creating the gap ourselves by not initially ensuring the conditions for all students to learn. The other problem is that we depend upon flawed, high-stakes testing as a credible measure of learning. Together, these two problems directly impact the resulting gaps that are gripping the world of factory schooling.

Multiple reform efforts over the years have tried to address the inadequacies of our current state of schooling affairs with little to no long-term or sustained success. Well-known and well-meaning individuals and groups have identified key issues, developed processes and practices, and offered some innovative ideas to hopefully reenergize, renew, and even reinvent schools as we know them.

They demand more accountability and transparency, less top-heavy management, and even business and entrepreneurial models that seem promising. Scores of books have been written lately explaining why schools are failing our children. Compelling documentaries and movies identify problems such as indifference, apathy, and, in some cases, poor teaching, especially in areas of high poverty.

Teachers typically enter the profession because they are drawn to working with and investing in young people, or they have a passion for learning themselves. Once entrapped in the system, they soon find that the structure is very confining and oftentimes detrimental to real learning. Most teachers follow the rules because their longevity in the field depends upon it.

Herein lies the most hideous deception that permeates the world of schooling today—that there is basically nothing we can do about it apart from yanking our kids out of mediocre schools and sending them to a better place. For many, this may not be an option. For some, it is their only hope.

Parents are increasingly demanding more for their children, more by way of special programs and opportunities in an effort to escape the doldrums of a regular classroom. Those who are fortunate enough to be in a school that is somewhat innovative may enjoy an environment that embraces and promotes out-of-the-box thinking. These opportunities are few and far between and rarely come under the publicly funded model. Why are so many parents searching for alternatives? Why do so many just accept the status quo?

There is a perspective held by many that explains the current system of schooling as an antiquated, industrial-aged model that no longer serves its intended purpose. In addition, the early history of schooling in the United States is one wrought with classism, racism, sexism, and gross inequities. Early on, public schools were for children of the white working class, which put immigrant, Native American, and black children at a great disadvantage. After years of legislated educational opportunities, we find these same groups still largely underserved and disenfranchised.

As early as 1779, Thomas Jefferson proposed a two-track system of schooling, one for the laborers and one for the learned. By the mid-1800s, agriculture gave way to manufacturing industries, which required a more skilled worker who could read, write, and perform basic arithmetic. Owners of industry needed a docile, obedient workforce and looked to public schools to provide it. Current schools in their present form are grossly inadequate to educate the future workforce.

This book meets a long-held need I've had to share my out-of-the-conventional-school-box ideas, hopes, and dreams. My hope is that this book will spark readers to venture out of their comfort zones and into a world of exciting possibilities—possibilities that enable, empower, and encourage them to think differently about the mainstream institution of school.

While I offer current research and voices who share my belief, I do speak from my own experiences and perspective in this book. I am keenly aware that others may not share that same perspective. However, as you read, ask yourself if the questions or ideas presented resonate with you. My desire is that everyone who reads this book will find a reawakening of passion, a morsel of hope, and a willingness to think out of the box when it comes to the world of formal schooling.

This, of course, will require the three Cs: courage, conviction, and commitment. It takes courage to question the status quo and confront the stark realities that exist in our schools. It takes conviction and determination to rediscover the joy and relevance in authentic learning. It takes commitment and resolve to be a voice and an active advocate for a much-needed change. Keep an open mind as we examine schooling in the following chapters.

ACKNOWLEDGMENTS

"Alone we can do so little; together we can do so much." —Helen Keller

The idea to write this book earned a spot on my bucket list in 2012. That is when I began, in earnest, to reflect on the fifty or so years that I have spent in schools. The force behind getting this book written and published came from my greatest encourager, Norm Rogers. Without his smile, honesty, and support, I never would have written *Learning Unleashed*. I know he, George, and my mom and dad are all looking down with great delight at this accomplishment. I miss them.

I needed the help of many to finally hold this book in my hand and to provide it to you, the reader. There are several to thank.

First, I want to thank my partners at Rowman & Littlefield: Tom Koerner, for believing that the message in my book is important enough to publish, and Bethany Janka and Hannah Fisher, for providing enormous support in bringing this book into its present form.

A small team of critical friends and family read my book and contributed greatly to the overall story. I am also thankful to the many children and adults who gave me honest and compelling testimonies of what and how they learned in school.

My children not only cheered me on in this endeavor but also provided me with constructive and practical support during this entire process. They are the reason I write with such passion. It is for them, my grandchildren, and children everywhere that I write this book.

I

"HOME" SCHOOL

"[Kids] don't remember what you try to teach them. They remember what you are." —Jim Henson, *It's Not Easy Being Green: And Other Things to Consider*

THE WONDER OF LEARNING

Have you ever watched a baby grabbing for a toy or rocking on all fours getting ready to lunge at a targeted destination? How about a toddler meticulously sorting blocks or pushing a dump truck twice her size across the room? Have you noticed how intently babies and young children observe facial expressions trying to mimic what they see? It is a fascinating study and one that is often overlooked in the hectic life of a modern-day family. What is true and apparent in these encounters with young children is a display of insatiable hunger and thirst for learning.

Research shows that babies can hear parents' voices inside the womb. Once born, a baby begins tuning into words and sentence patterns to figure out what's being said. Infants also have great powers of observation as they begin to understand and learn about some of the more complicated things—like love, trust, time, and cause and effect—that exist in their physical and emotional world.

Children around three years old typically have a vocabulary of about two hundred words, and they use them to navigate their world. They are innately curious and intrigued with the sound of the spoken word as well as the facial expressions and emotions attached to those words.

They learn from carefully observing the caring adults in their lives. It is simply amazing to watch the organic and monumental learning that happens between birth and five years old.

Sight, sound, taste, touch, and smell all play harmoniously in the sensory processing of young children. The five senses are firing up every waking moment as little ones interact with their environment. They stretch their capacity to learn in every situation, relying on those senses to process this exciting world in which they now live.

Because children have an innate capacity to mimic what they see and hear, these early years are an optimal time for them to learn languages other than their own. This is very doable, as evidenced in many countries abroad. As a country in general, Americans hesitate and sometimes fear learning a new language. They are uncomfortable making mistakes and are not confident enough in their ability to comprehend and pronounce words correctly.

This is not the case with children. They love echoing what they hear, even if it comes out wrong. In fact, making up similar sounding words that rhyme often brings sheer delight to little ones as they repeat them over and over. They discover how empowering the spoken word is.

If a child is fortunate enough to live in a diverse neighborhood, they greatly benefit from exposure to those various cultures, languages, and traditions. Likewise, if in their immediate or extended family different ethnicities, races, or languages exist, they are likely to possess a much richer view of their world than those who may not have that opportunity. Trying new foods, listening to family stories, and participating in traditions from other cultures or ethnicities provide a rich experience that can't be learned any other way.

When children are given an opportunity to learn about the world around them in an authentic manner, they build strong learning bridges that lead them to new and exciting discoveries down the road. Before bias and prejudice enter their construct of life, they are wildly enthusiastic about learning anything new or different. It is apparent that adults are not typically this enthusiastic. What happens?

TECHNOLOGY THAT TEACHES

While it still holds some influence in the overall development of a young person, television is no longer the only game in town. Selective television programming can inform and take us to parts unknown while providing interesting lessons in science, history, and the arts. However, the current heavy hitter by way of technology is anything handheld, connected to the web, easily accessed, and portable.

When monitored and chosen carefully, communication technology has great potential as an avenue for learning. It can serve as a catalyst, sparking creativity and innovation within the mind of the user. However, when consumed in massive, repetitive, and random doses, it can also become an addictive escape, rendering its victims powerless to the real world of imagination. Gaming has developed into a mind-numbing kryptonite targeting our youngest and most vulnerable. A consumerist mind-set, driven by the almighty dollar, is taking an entire generation hostage without a shred of conscience. Consumers beware!

While it may help to develop small motor skills or keen eye-hand coordination for younger children, playing a game on an iPad or other interactive device does not require the user to access the same type of reasoning skills as an authentic, real-life challenge does. Calling it learning is a stretch at best. Rather, it may provide reinforcement to specific skills being learned such as identifying numbers, letters, colors, etc.

When watching a toddler, one can easily observe the repeated trial-and-error method in many of their daily routines. Play and discovery are rewarding avenues of learning. Children learn to persevere, to grapple with varying levels of difficulty, and, ultimately, to realize how things work. Imagination, innovation, and creativity are the keys to real learning opportunities. Younger children do this instinctively, which is something to keep in mind as they enter formal schooling.

EARLY READING

Children innately enjoy hearing a good story and they look forward to hearing it more than once. When a child knows that this enjoyment comes from being close with someone they trust and interacting with something called a book, it effortlessly transports them to both known and unknown worlds. The sheer delight on the faces of little ones as they hear their favorite story (or a new one) is forever etched on the minds and hearts of the person lucky enough to witness this.

Some parents proudly proclaim that their children can read at three years old when they find them easily repeating the words they've heard in their favorite storybook as they turn each page. This is a prime example of how familiarity through frequent interaction breeds success. There may, or may not, be true comprehension occurring at this early age. However, children know that there is a code to crack, and over time, they will naturally develop that code themselves.

The more exposure to written language for sheer enjoyment, the better chance a child will seek this out as they grow older. The curiosity one is born with can be either nurtured and supported or stifled and suppressed. Providing a child with frequent and enjoyable exposure to books, words, and the illustrations that accompany them is an awesome responsibility. Building a young child's library can have a lasting impact on their future learning.

CREATIVE AND PERFORMING ARTS

At a very early age, children discover the beauty in their world through varying hues of prism colors, musical rhythms and patterns, and kinesthetic movement that brings sheer ecstasy to their bodies. The word *intoxicating* comes to mind. Again, observing a little one lost in a world of creative and performing arts is a delightful sight to behold. The body swaying, the melody oozing from their little voices, the colorful costumes they use for dress up, and the artwork they proudly gift us all indicate that something incredibly spectacular is happening.

For a young child, this is a natural expression and interaction with a miraculous world of stunning possibilities—a world not yet touched by the harsh realities of life. This is the world of a child who is growing in a safe, caring, and nurturing environment. Their eyes are their canvasses, ready for color, light, dance, expression, and meaning. They are the artists, and we supply their tools. Whatever their minds can perceive they can create without any notion of perfection, mistakes, or competition. Those concepts are not yet in their repertoire.

How powerful this creativity is and how important it is for caring adults to come alongside a child to facilitate this natural interaction with their world. By the way, creativity does not wane as one ages. If it appears to lose prominence, it is more likely due to the world of schooling in which they will soon enter. Its obvious lack of prominence there contributes to the overall decrease of interest and perceived lack of importance in the schooling arena. Huge missed opportunities make way for unwanted behaviors that sometimes manifest themselves as boredom, distractibility, and rebellion. Robbing a child of this natural gift by substituting it for more academic pursuits is a travesty. This should not be an either/or proposition.

WORK ETHIC AND RESPONSIBILITY

How does one instill the value of a good work ethic and responsibility in a four-year-old? It happens more naturally than one would expect. Picking up toys after play, helping with chores, and learning to dress and care for oneself are precursors to transitioning into BIG people life. True, this may not be a child's favorite activity, but it certainly is critical for overall healthy growth and development. Responsibility in metered doses enables a young child to become independent, self-sufficient, and reliable. These are important character traits that will pay huge dividends down the road.

Many children find that being helpful and responsible is gratifying, and they often seek opportunities to demonstrate these traits. As they mature, the level of responsibility mirrors their capacity to work. Contributing to the household in which they live is a stepping-stone to a greater realization that their neighborhood, city, and eventually, world, are also places where they can ultimately contribute.

Teaching children how to give is one of the best lessons in work ethic and responsibility. It helps them understand that when they give their time, energy, talents, and even finances to help or serve someone else, they are investing in something much larger than themselves. Working as a family to help others is one of the best ways to model this kind of giving.

Many children will think of this intuitively and suggest that their family help a stray dog, a friend who appears hungry, or an elderly neighbor in need of assistance. Working to help someone else removes "what do I get out of this" from the equation. It provides a young person with a rewarding sense of intrinsic value.

NUMBER SENSE

Numbers are everywhere, and young children instinctively love them. They joyfully count even before anyone gives them words to use such as *one*, *two*, and *three*. They visually count using their fingers, their Legos, or their blocks. They observe the number of crackers on their plate, they hear the number of times something is repeated, and they look for patterns of regularity with daily routines.

In addition, a child's exposure to a variety of music deeply solidifies counting, pattern seeking, and regularities. All of these experiences prepare them for the more complicated and higher expressions of mathematics.

Questions like *why*, *how much*, and *how many* seem to be hardwired into a little one's vocabulary almost as soon as they can speak. Hearing words like *a million*, *a zillion*, or even exaggerated ones like *kagillion* or *bajillion* seems to fascinate little ones as they ponder the immensity of those terms. What is happening in the mind of a four- or five-year-old when they consider the world of numbers? Watch their faces and be astounded.

Rarely do they appear to be overwhelmed, frightened, or bored. In fact, they are anxious and intent on learning everything they can about numbers and their meaning—so much so that they teach themselves basic concepts like addition, subtraction, and greater than and less than without the assistance of an adult. Watching a young child separating items in groups and putting them back together again based on their perceived likenesses or differences is simply an amazing observation.

As they near school age, their fascination with math is at an all-time high. Children who have not yet experienced any kind of structured schooling are in for a surprise. Apart from the initial exposure in kindergarten, learning math in school has the potential to become a less than stellar experience and one that may conjure up anxiety and frustration. Far from the joy it used to provide, many children in school learn to endure it. Why is this the case?

PHYSICAL MOVEMENT

From the time they are born, and well into their early years, a child's body is in perpetual motion. Children first learn how to control their hands and feet and then build the capacity to direct their bodies to do whatever comes to mind. Movement soon becomes automatic as they intently concentrate on gross and fine motor skills. Clumsy attempts to carry items much larger than themselves eventually make way to selecting crayons—first with their fists, and then with the index finger and thumb. Children grow in confidence as they become more adept at grasping items within their reach. It empowers them.

Movement is essential for healthy growth, and children who are given that opportunity will thrive. Ensuring that exercise and outdoor activities are part of a child's daily routine provides them with not only health benefits but an opportunity to build greater stamina. When neighborhood playgrounds are accessible, the lessons learned there with other children are irreplaceable.

Before entering school, children spend the majority of the day on their feet. When they do sit, it is momentary at best. It's been said that children can attend for as many minutes as they are old. For example, a four-year-old can sit for an activity for approximately four minutes, and so forth, commensurate with their age. It is, therefore, not surprising that they are not prepared for long periods of sit time when they start school. Yet, that is exactly what we expect from them.

RESOURCEFULNESS, COMPASSION, AND RESPECT

Modeling resourcefulness, compassion, and respect starts with the daily interaction between parent and child. Children learn from observing everything you say and do. No doubt, this is a very heavy responsibility for the parent, and exceptionally difficult when facing any kind of adversity. It is good to remind yourself that adversity comes in many forms and at unexpected times. Having an arsenal of strategies tucked away in our minds for retrieval as needed will definitely help. Pick the strategies that work best for you.

For those who face an uphill climb by virtue of their circumstances, having help with this task of parenting in some way may help alleviate the feeling of overload. As adults, we often find ourselves dealing with adult-sized issues in which we can choose to be overwhelmed, or we can choose to overcome. As the adage implies, make lemonade when you've been given lemons.

Regardless of how difficult the day might be, it is important to note that children are not lemons! Treat them with compassion and respect and model for them the art of resourcefulness. Children who learn this at home have a greater chance of surviving at school. There they will surely face a lack of resources and may encounter little compassion or respect for differences among their schoolmates.

LEARNING VERSUS SCHOOLING

Learning, for most children, comes by way of authentic and meaningful experiences. It often involves others but can sometimes only involve the child. Neighborhoods, families, other cultures, languages, and technology all play a part in understanding the world around us. Learning happens from observing, experimenting, making mistakes, and persevering. The natural process of learning is amazing and unique to each child.

Processing and thinking through difficult situations and problems is very different for each young person. Tackling a challenge or assessing a threat is also very unique and depends upon what has been seen, heard, and learned very early in life. Even with genetic predispositions, individuals bring their own set of eyes with which to see and process the world.

Navigating independence is not only important to a child's growth, but an essential element in the "learning" process. It's only by "doing something ourselves" that we really comprehend what we are trying to learn. Doing something ourselves implies perseverance, multiple attempts, and a genuine sense of accomplishment. How often do we hear little ones scold us with the admonition, "I want to do this by myself" as they struggle with something we'd just prefer to do *for* them?

The basis for learning still remains the home and what happens during the first five years of a child's life and thereafter. While some assert that access to preschool will level the playing field, there is nothing that can replace a loving, strong, and nurturing home life. Nothing ever will. In spite of less than optimal circumstances, children love to learn and generally develop coping skills to survive.

Young children, for the most part, are eager to start school. They are anxious to access more information in which to learn about the world. They know it means meeting new friends, being away from home for a long period of time, and having a really cool backpack. What they often don't know is that their learning will now depend upon how well they listen, repeat, attend, and perform. They will be programmed, bribed, confused, and herded. There is nothing authentic or natural about it.

School for many will start off as an exciting adventure full of interesting surprises and great fun. Typically, by third grade most of these children, if asked, will describe a completely different scenario than the one heard about at the beginning of their schooling journey. What happens and why? An important takeaway in the next few chapters is to remember that "schooling" does not necessarily equate to getting a good education. *Schooling is what is done to us, and becoming educated is what we do for ourselves.*

2

THE KINDERGARTEN EXPERIMENT

"School was pretty hard for me at the beginning. My mother taught me how to read before I got to school and so when I got there I really just wanted to do two things. I wanted to read books because I loved reading books and I wanted to go outside and chase butterflies. You know, do the things that five-year-olds like to do. I encountered authority of a different kind than I had ever encountered before, and I did not like it. And they really almost got me. They came close to really beating any curiosity out of me." —Steve Jobs

AND SO IT BEGAN

Kindergarten entered the United States in the mid-1800s based on the work of Friedrich Froebel, a German educator. His philosophy resonated with many who saw the need to provide early opportunities for young children. In the United States, most of these young ones were the children of laborers who needed child care during the day.[1]

> [Froebel] believed that humans are essentially productive and creative, and that fulfillment comes through developing these in harmony with God and the world. His vision was to stimulate an appreciation and love for children, to provide a new but small world for children to play with their age group and experience their first gentle taste of independence. His kindergarten system consisted of games and songs, construction, and gifts and occupations. The play materials were what he called gifts and the activities were occupations. His

system allowed children to compare, test, and explore. His philosophy also consisted of four basic components which were free self-activity, creativity, social participation, and motor expression.[2]

As the idea of kindergarten caught on, it also experienced a slow metamorphosis from Froebel's foundations to a more academically based program. Over the years and even more recently, kindergarten programs have become more rigorous than in the past. They have also become fully integrated into the regular school programs serving children in both private and public venues K–12.[3]

In a September 19, 2014, *EdWeek* article, the writer, Christina Samuels, referenced the Denver-based Education Commission of the States, noting that "just 15 states require students to attend kindergarten." The commission reports the following:

> Such laws reflect a disconnect between state policy and the importance of kindergarten, which some researchers are calling the "new 1st grade," with its increased focus on literacy and accountability for the youngest school children. The Common Core State Standards also treat kindergarten as a full-fledged grade, without reference to the fact that for some children, kindergarten may be fewer than 15 hours per week.[4]

According to researchers Daphna Bassok, Scott Latham, and Anna Rorem from the University of Virginia, in their working paper titled *Is Kindergarten the New First Grade?*, they highlight important evidence that points to the dramatic shift in the kindergarten emphasis over the years. In the same *EdWeek* article, the writer shares the findings of the University of Virginia researchers:

> From 1998 to 2006, kindergarten teachers reported devoting 25 percent more time to teaching early literacy, increasing it to 7 hours per week, the researchers found. In 1998, a little less than a third of teachers said that kindergartners should leave the grade knowing how to read. By 2006, that percentage had risen to 65 percent. The researchers also noted a corresponding drop in other elements of kindergarten, such as social studies, music, art, and physical education.[5]

These findings are alarming on many fronts. Both state school systems and their respective lawmakers are either grossly out of touch with well-researched child and adolescent development theory and practices, or they just don't care. Legislated mandates such as forced kindergarten attendance is a blatant act of tyranny. Unfortunately, at least fifteen states do not agree.

The intense shift toward academics and the required successful completion of grade-level standards has placed kindergarten-aged children in the direct line of fire. The expectation that all kindergarten children will master the same given standards in different time scenarios (full day, extended day, and half day) is ludicrous. An arbitrary nine- or ten-month grade-level cut-off requirement is the antithesis of sound developmental learning.

Parents who have the option whether to register their child in kindergarten often welcome this choice as a parental right. That right, however, is taken away as compulsory schooling takes over in first grade. Many parents choose to exercise their homeschooling rights as an alternative method of learning. Even then, most states demand a certain level of compliance and reporting to ensure that children are indeed learning something.

KINDERGARTEN ENTRANCE

This rite-of-passage ceremony occurs every year with millions of little ones entering the school yards across the United States. Some are clinging fearfully to their parents, and others stand quietly looking a bit frightened as they wait for a signal to start school. Anxious parents lovingly accompany their children into the classroom, where the process of disengagement begins. Frequently, tears, whimpers, and general apprehension take over as the children size up the situation to determine whether this place is safe and the person in charge looks like someone they might trust.

Some intuitive kindergarten teachers who fully understand sound child development practices have already visited the homes of these children to introduce themselves and meet the families. This helps to lower apprehension and fear of the unknown that can occur on the first day of school. Many schools offer a designated day for parents and students to visit their classroom before school starts to become familiar with their new surroundings. For most, this may be the first time they are meeting their teacher.

The teacher eventually signals to the parents that they must leave, reassuring them that all is well and their children will be fine. Parents take the cue, whispering their good-byes and "be good"s to their children, reassuring them. Mass exiting of parents from tearful children is an alarming sight but apparently one that must occur in order to get on with the schooling of the children. Once parents are gone, but not forgotten, the teacher gathers students together, oftentimes on the carpeted floor, to establish the necessary routines.

To a little one, the room seems massive with very high ceilings and lots of nooks and crannies filled with interesting items. In a quick scan, they survey books, perhaps a chalkboard, cubbies, art centers, and the teacher's desk. In some cases, they will also find computers or a large-screen TV for viewing. Some of these classrooms provide an unobstructed window view of a compact playground on either a blacktop or chipped bark. In time, most children enter willingly, lining up at the door and marching into the big room that they call kindergarten.

After a few days of school, it becomes apparent that school is quite different than home. As time passes, the novelty of school begins to wear off, shifting more toward a familiar daily routine. These routines include frequent practice at properly walking and getting in line, raising hands, copying from the board or book, and tracing or filling out something called worksheets. It typically also includes hearing a good story, coloring or painting, and counting colored rods or blocks.

Occasionally these activities are interrupted with a cool field trip, a quick recess break, or a classroom visitor. Some classrooms play music, enlist helpers, and allow frequent playtime; some don't. It all depends upon the teacher, the curriculum, and the bell schedule. In some cases, there are well over twenty-five children sharing space with a teacher and loads of furniture. It can be a very busy looking place with little to no room for stretching or movement.

In spite of less than optimal conditions, most children learn to navigate the physical and emotional world of school and all that it entails. Kindergarten is designed to provide a five-year-old with structure and predictability while they learn what is required of them. They are programmed fairly quickly on the requirements and given praise when they succeed without incident.

WHY IS MOVEMENT SO IMPORTANT?

In the October 2015 *Journal of American Academy of Pediatrics*, recent research found that children who were involved in a regular physical activity program showed important enhancement of cognitive performance and brain function. The findings, according to University of Illinois professor Charles Hillman and colleagues,

> demonstrate a causal effect of a physical program on executive control, and provide support for physical activity for improving childhood cognition and brain health. If it seems odd that this is something that still needs support, that's because it is odd, yes. Physical activity is clearly a high, high-yield investment for all kids, but especially those attentive or hyperactive. This brand of research is still published and written about as though it were a novel finding, in part because exercise programs for kids remain underfunded and underprioritized in many school curricula, even though exercise is clearly integral to maximizing the utility of time spent in class.[6]

Apart from the short recess periods and some occasional out-of-seat activities, kindergarteners are rather stationary beings in their classrooms. In observational terms, watching a loud, energetic, and interactive bunch of children within a classroom can send two different messages. One may consider this an out-of-control, noisy, and unproductive environment, and it may very well be. Through another set of eyes, one might witness authentic learning, trial-and-error processing, and persevering and creating under the skilled facilitation of an insightful and dynamic teacher.

As days turn into weeks and the weeks into months, learning becomes a repetitive and necessary routine. When observed, one might see some students rapidly finishing assigned work, those who take a while longer, and many who fall somewhere along the continuum. In some cases, the finished product may or may not provide an accurate reflection of learning.

Think about a child who is asked to sit in school for a good portion of the day. No wonder the teacher finds several of them popping up frequently, lying or rolling on the floors, tapping a pencil, or rocking in their chairs. Sitting too long can be a prison sentence for many young children who learn best as they stand. Yet this is done on a regular basis every day in schools.

Savvy teachers have discovered and utilize frequent stand-and-stretch breaks as a way to help break up the monotony of sitting for hours. However, the very structure of a small classroom with too many children and too much furniture limits the chances for any substantial movement. Movement is mostly determined by the teacher. Distracted and jittery children are a given when there is no allowance for needed and frequent movement.

WELCOME TO THE INSTITUTION OF SCHOOL: YOU'RE GOING TO LIKE IT HERE, WE PROMISE

Massive amounts of time are spent looking at the teacher explaining subject concepts. Students are then asked to practice on paper what they've just heard. Then they are assigned homework that is more of the same. The cycle is repeated every day until the day it becomes a test—one that they must complete with accuracy. Occasionally, amazing teachers will veer from the textbook and worksheets to allow for more hands-on activities and discussion that provide multiple exposures to the concept being taught. This is a refreshing departure from the norm and a welcomed opportunity for students who delight in learning this way.

Unfortunately, school textbooks do not allow for teacher creativity or autonomy because the final test is written based on the previous pages in the book. Teachers fear veering off too much as it may not represent the vocabulary and design of the test. They often take the safe route and stick to what is in the book whether or not a child is having success with it. They know that the test data is the accepted litmus for learning.

Periodically teachers will band together in spite of the rigidity of a textbook series and develop their own approach based on the specific needs of students in their classrooms. What a delight when this occurs, when children are given the respect and opportunity to learn in a way that helps them naturally grow. Of course, many schools and districts demand strict adherence to the same textbooks, curriculum, and lesson types. This often handcuffs bright and creative teachers who instinctively know that there are multiple ways to present and share information. Children learn differently. How can we expect all of them to fit into the textbook design?

Listening and observing for a few hours in a kindergarten classroom provide a revealing glimpse of a five-year-old child's thought processes regarding school—what they are actually doing and why they are doing it. A question that produces a most intriguing array of responses but is rarely asked is this: "How do you know that you've learned what was just taught?" Typically, no one ever asks them that specific question.

Questions usually fall along the lines of "What are you learning today?" Sometimes they can tell you and sometimes they have difficulty articulating it clearly. Most times they will generalize and respond with a subject header like math or reading.

When teachers deeply understand the importance of constructive and immediate formative feedback and take the necessary time to provide it, it is more likely that a student will, in fact, learn from that encounter and be able to respond clearly and specifically regarding what and how they are learning.

Contrary to what teachers have been told or directed to do, it is less important to see a written standard or objective on the board and more impactful hearing a student demonstrate and explain what they are learning. It is powerful and meaningful when a student can tell you the specific steps they used to solve a problem or the meaning and usage of words in a story. By the way, this can happen in kindergarten classrooms.

The promise of "you are going to like it here" sometimes falls short of its intended outcome. The "institution of school" looms larger than life and is all-consuming. It spills over into home time via required homework. It demands long attention spans and astute listening skills. It observes strict time limits and reinforces them as needed. It offers little opportunity for creativity and innovation as textbooks and most classroom materials are designed to be done at a desk with paper and pencil. It determines when students are hungry and food is served, when bathroom breaks are needed, and when the rooms are too cold or too hot. It determines how quickly and effectively learning is occurring as measured by frequent tests that are given grades.

Most children don't question these happenings much beyond some pause and bewilderment. They learn how to follow the rules, play the game, and most of the time pay attention. Being comfortable asking curious questions at home becomes an apprehensive effort at school. Now, there are only right questions to go along with the correct answers. In school, choice is rarely allowed, and what is done for the hours a child attends is mostly determined by the teacher.

However, as malleable minors, little ones oblige learning this mechanical routine to the teacher's delight. A few refuse to be herded and end up sitting in the time-out chair or facing the wall for their obvious misbehavior. Some children never catch on to the routines and end up out of the classroom more than in it. A teacher rarely has time to deal with these students during class time and, therefore, must remove them in order to keep the other students orderly and on task. What has the child learned in this scenario? For some, getting to leave the classroom becomes their escape and reward.

A NEEDED MAKEOVER

Learning is organic, unique, and different for each child, and, more important, fueled by interest, creativity, and curiosity. Children learn and grow at different rates in different ways. Some grow more quickly in one area than in another. Some learn best with others; some do better on their own. What better way to kill that innate creativity and curiosity than to package learning into a rigidly constructed box governed by a strict sense of time, space, and logistics? The joy of learning soon becomes lost when it is prepackaged, force-fed, and highly restrictive.

In the past, kindergarten was mostly about learning to follow directions, play nicely, and color within the lines. It was a place where children made new friends and painted some awesome pictures. It was also where recognizing and using letters and numbers led to reading, writing, and simple mathematics.

Over the years, experts in the field have staked out firmly held territories with regard to what kind of learning is best during these younger years. Some believe there is good reason to heavily emphasize academics given the amount and depth of standards and topics that must be covered. Many parents are strong supporters of this approach, proudly proclaiming that their children learned to read in preschool and need to be challenged in kindergarten or they will become bored. They also tend to support all-day kindergarten programs.

Others say that children naturally learn if given the right environment, a facilitative teacher, and enough time to explore their world. They believe in and value extended time for play and opportunities for more authentic learning opportunities. They prefer kindergarten experiences that foster creativity and imagination. Parents who support this more gradual approach to learning often tend to prefer a shorter-day kindergarten program.

For the most part, parents know their children best. They know what makes them tick or, in some cases, what makes them explode. They are usually aware of how well their children have navigated their first five years dealing with conflict, attention span, learning preferences, and social and emotional stability.

Unfortunately, most schools and school systems are not democracies. Kindergarten classrooms are not democratically organized, and the teachers are not voted in by the parents or community. Likewise, the curriculum is prescribed and inflexible. The schedule is unyielding, and the number of children in the classroom is predetermined by someone else. A multitude of parents wish they had more of a say in these matters. After all, up to this point in time they have made every important decision concerning their children. They are gradually weaned from being heavily involved to supporting the teacher and school in this endeavor.

For a child, kindergarten may be one of their best school experiences or it can prove to be a difficult journey ending in epic failure. In the case of the latter, it may require the student to do it all over again, hoping for better results. This is not sound practice, yet we do it with regularity, hoping that as they mature they will catch on to school. Some learn the system; others don't. Casualties are inevitable.

3

EIGHT YEARS OF *THIS*?

"In a word, learning is decontextualized. We break ideas down into tiny pieces that bear no relation to the whole. We give students a brick of information, followed by another brick, followed by another brick, until they are graduated, at which point we assume they have a house. What they have is a pile of bricks, and they don't have it for long." —Alfie Kohn

ACQUIRED ACQUIESCENCE

As time passes, students learn that compliance and attentiveness will ensure their success in school. This is what many young children strive to do without much complaint. They begin to realize that learning in school is the result of how well they've listened and are able to repeat back verbatim. For some, this is a challenging feat as they often struggle with memorization, which seems to be most of what they do in school.

As students traverse each grade level, various school "subjects" are scheduled throughout the day. Lunch and recess provide a welcomed opportunity to finally talk, laugh, and play with schoolmates. When asked their favorite subject in school, a frequent and common response from young children is *recess*. Occasionally, art or Physical Education may enter the mix of favorites, but to a lesser degree. Ever wonder why this is the case? Recess, while still somewhat restrictive, allows for some freedom of choice and, more important, movement. Both are critical to a healthy and well-balanced learning experience.

Students are grouped by age, given a definitive time frame in which to complete the mandated curriculum, and rewarded with good grades and forward movement if successful. However, child psychologists generally agree that human beings grow and develop at different rates. They also tell us that given enough time, proper tools, and a conducive environment, all children can learn. They point out that the brain is hardwired to learn much more than is typically expected. With this information readily available and part of a teacher's knowledge base, why do we ignore it in schools and place arbitrary time frames and restrictions on learning?

Children's brains are sensory-seeking organs constantly trying to make meaning of the environment in which they live. The brain looks for patterns, familiarity, novelties, and ways in which to solve problems. Neurons are firing at a rapid pace to make new connections when given new information. Interacting through the five senses is critical to learning and so is experimentation and trial and error. Children at five, eight, or even twelve years old are constantly observing, processing, and problem solving.

For the most part, schools systematically train students to do the opposite. Children are rarely asked to use their own powers of observation, problem solving, or intuition. Instead, they are taught to regurgitate information in typically one format. They are trained to properly complete worksheets and study guides. They are directed to prove what they know on a test. This is how school works, whether effective or not.

EARLY YEARS

In the lower elementary school setting, there is usually one teacher who presents separate lessons for each subject that is taught. Each lesson follows a predetermined sequence that often lasts about twenty or thirty minutes. It can't last longer than that because teachers have to teach several other subjects during the day. Students are not given more time to grapple with a new concept because there is no more time. Ask any teacher in any classroom across the United States, and they will unanimously agree that *more time* is what they and their students need.

Yet, we continue to schedule subjects and create lesson plans that mirror what the textbook says. Although this may be a somewhat exaggerated example, it is not that far from reality. A week or two may be allocated for learning addition and another week or two for learning subtraction. There are multiple days of brief classroom practice with assigned homework, followed by a test. Moving on to the next round of lessons is the goal, and the schedule reinforces this. There is definitely a pattern in this scenario, but not one that will yield real or lasting learning. These are just bricks of information.

These bricks are not used to build a solid house of understanding or knowledge. However, they are always gathered together on a test, sometimes recognizable to the student and sometimes not. They are deemed to be mastered as evidenced in a passing grade, or they are lost forever in an irretrievable heap of failing and irreversible grades. Time is fleeting, so there is no going back to square one.

A certain sinking feeling occurs for many young ones who are doomed to that place of no return. It escapes them unless some willing adult recognizes this mishap and, instead of marking them a failure, decides to *reteach* the lesson in a way that the student can understand. After all, isn't learning the whole point of going to school?

In our current schooling format, there are multiple subjects and not enough time to reteach all of them for those who did not comprehend. So what is the answer? Often schools create and provide their version of a remedy called *intervention support*. Sadly, interventions depend upon scheduling, timing of lunch and recess, and whether or not materials and people are available.

Many times these interventions are a repeat of the same with more worksheets to complete. Rarely are they utilizing a different approach or identifying only the specific types of errors that are found for each individual child. Occasionally this does happen when a teacher takes the time to target specific areas of perceived weakness and offers the child a differently tailored lesson. This redemption happens when the teacher is determined to see every child succeed.

The opposite problem exists as well. Children who may grasp concepts quickly and are ready to move on may find themselves stuck in a holding pattern. They are often given busywork, extra reading time, or other random assignments while waiting for those who may need more time. There is a certain dynamic tension between the two, which exacerbates the problem. Instead of yielding to one set of students or the other, the system averages it out and no one gets the pace they need.

Teachers know this all too well. Even amid all their efforts, they tend to teach in the middle. This frequent practice falsely assumes that all the children in the class will have a shot at learning. They don't.

The individualized attention that a family provides is impossible in factory schooling. Both slower and faster learners are frustrated. Even within the same child one may encounter a greater aptitude for math than for reading or vice versa. This child may need less time for learning the math and more time to access reading. Unfortunately, the way school works, individualized time for learning is not allowed. The school sets rigid schedules, and the students are held captive.

LATER YEARS

In the middle school years, ages eleven to thirteen, we typically segregate children from their younger counterparts. We are told this is mostly due to the hormonal influences that seem to wreak havoc in the bodies and minds of young adolescents. These children often find themselves in one of two camps.

There are those who managed to make it through the K–5 or K–6 schooling maze and are gearing up for more of the same. Others who did not fare as well during the early school years are in for the ride of their lives. An internal battle rages as they straddle an ever increasingly difficult curriculum coupled with the inability to determine what they are really good at in school. These difficulties, along with the ever perplexing dilemma of what to wear to school on any given day, create uncertainty and, in many cases, anxiety. It is a pivotal time for sure.

The intensity of emotions seems to be at an all-time high during these years. Friends and relationships are the focus of most conversations, while academics and "schoolwork" seem to take a backseat. Confidence and body image are at an all-time low mostly due to external factors. As the body is experiencing rapid growth and change, proper rest, exercise, and diet are a must. Yet this rarely occurs, often sabotaging an otherwise alert and interested young mind.

In these school years, we typically ask children to start school early, roam an expansive campus with hundreds of other students, and get to their assigned class on time with a different teacher for each subject they are required to take. We then increase classroom numbers by ten or more students regardless of the room size. Learning to navigate this paradigm is daunting at best, but most of the middle schoolers catch on fairly quickly.

They traverse the campuses in masses by grade levels usually without incident. However, the sheer volume of animated young people moving in different directions guarantees that someone, somewhere in that mix will deviate, disrupt, or detach. It is often believed that large groups of students sometimes create a mob mentality, which requires strict monitoring. So, we station several adults across the campus to ensure order and smooth movement. This is a not-so-delightful exercise for the adults and an annoying intrusion into the ill-conceived belief by some young adolescents that they deserve more trust and privacy.

For those young people who are not able to process the massive amount of new information presented by five or more different teachers in the given time frame, interventions are introduced. Effective interventions at middle school are virtually nonexistent due to the rigid and unyielding rapid pace of instruction, testing, and moving on to the next topic. When interventions are offered, they are served up on an unsavory platter of more study sheets and book work.

How does one ever get caught up? The depressing side effects of middle school interventions is the substantial loss of something else the student enjoys doing and the stigma attached to needing an intervention in the first place. Unfortunately, factory schooling in its current version does not provide enough time, enough resources, or enough teacher training and autonomy to adequately tackle this ongoing problem.

However, the underlying root of the problem is not the fault of the student. It lies squarely in the system's unyielding structure. This is a structure that holds children hostage to a prescribed set of arbitrary deadlines. It strangles learners with an unrelated and boring curriculum that often inhibits and restricts any ongoing authentic learning opportunities. Why do we do this repeatedly without giving it a second thought?

SQUARE PEG, ROUND HOLE REVISITED

Reading, writing, and basic arithmetic were the tenets, and loading classrooms in batches mimicked the factories. That is exactly what happened all over the country. Schools became "Fact Factories" as Alfie Kohn describes in his book, *The Schools Our Children Deserve*. When we needed factory workers, they were provided via our schooling system.[1]

Sir Ken Robinson tells us that there are three principles upon which our educational systems are based: conformity, compliance, and familiarity. He adds that we should have systems based on diversity.[2]

Long after the need for factory workers, our schools still operated under that premise. Not much has changed even now. Factory schooling cannot possibly account for all the individual learning needs of each student; therefore, everyone loses. If we simply understood and began to practice sound pedagogy, the damage that our school constructs are having on our children would be reversed. There are many ways this can happen.

One of the most effective shifts would be less didactic teaching, where students sit as receptacles of the teacher's knowledge passively listening in order to learn. Most times, this just becomes a monologue in which students may or may not be interested. They have little to no input or real involvement apart from an occasional teacher question or directive to complete an assignment.

Even with all the push for more interactive lessons and use of technology to access information, the bulk of what still happens in most classrooms on a regular basis is a disproportionate amount of teacher talk as opposed to student and student or student and teacher interaction. However, in those classrooms where teachers fully embrace and practice an authentic engagement philosophy, one might see and hear something quite different. Again, this is hit or miss depending upon the teacher's professional development experiences and comfort level with this kind of teaching. The sheer volume of students is also a key factor.

There are many school reformers, educational experts, researchers, and such who have tried to offer strategies, programs, and structures in an effort to *fix* the problems we encounter in our schools. However, fixing the problem by adding another layer on top of a building whose foundation is crumbling is risky at best. If a house's foundation is faulty, it never stabilizes or gets better over time no matter what fixes are applied. The only way to keep it from falling and causing severe damage is to raze the house and totally redo the foundation.

Reformers and policy makers don't often suggest this drastic remedy because it would alter the cosmic forces and wreak havoc on state, federal, and local school systems that know only one way to do this thing called school. Many believe that major foundational or structural change is tampering with the unknown and totally unnecessary. It is deemed much more effective to just mandate change and hope for the best.

Yanking the school system from its roots is too radical and risky. That would imply that something has failed and continues to fail. It would also presume that there is a better system than the one we currently promote. It would require consensus, which is never easy, especially when it comes to schooling in this country. It would mean a system that can hold its own and stand up to the politics, rhetoric, and nonsense that have become the fabric of schools for the past one hundred years. No wonder we apply quick fixes. It's so much easier.

Imagine a groundswell of citizens demanding the razing and restructuring of every school that is not working for its students. What are the implications of that mandate? How might that play out in neighborhoods where schools are not effectively facilitating learning? Many have tried to tackle this beast, and some have emerged as beacons of hope in the midst of great despair. Again, systemically, these are drops in a leaking bucket. We can only hope for better on behalf of our children.

Utopia, some might say. Not feasible or possible, others will declare. Better to just throw strings-attached money to schools and judge how well they pull themselves out of the muck. Create more laws and place more restrictions on school systems to perform and that will ensure our children are competitive with counterparts around the world. We offer excuse after excuse why our children are not learning, knowing that within a few short schooling years we have irreversibly altered their inquisitive and miraculous minds with our rigid and overbearing school agendas. More important, if we just mandate learning it will happen.

Is anyone else concerned about this horrific abdication of responsibility for the overall welfare, freedom, and knowledge base of the next generation? Apparently, those sitting at the state and federal power level seem to paint a much different picture of schooling—one that indoctrinates the masses in propaganda blitzes to assure Americans that our schools and programs are world class. At the same time, an ever increasing number of students are dropping off the school grid, choosing alternative methods to become educated.

4

NEIGHBORHOODS: A LOST OASIS

"If everyone invested in the neighborhood they lived in, the United States would be a magical place." —Anthony Mackie

WEALTH OF OPPORTUNITIES

Outside of school there are multiple opportunities for extended learning. Savvy parents and children often take advantage of them. Many of them are free while others may require a fee to participate. As many parents find themselves working Monday through Friday, these types of opportunities are often accessed after school or on the weekends. A weekly calendar can fill up quickly with little to no time for much else. When you add homework to the mix, it becomes even more challenging.

Homeschooled children have the advantage of accessing these learning experiences at any time, one of the many benefits that homeschooling affords. Homeschoolers can pack up and take off to the museum, the library, the fire station, or the aquarium without worrying about getting back to the school bus by one o'clock. They can choose to go back again the next day if they want to or they can head in a totally different direction. Many homeschoolers enjoy a co-op day, where they meet with other homeschoolers for classes they choose to take based on an interest or area of study.

While a strong and dedicated commitment is needed, homeschooling offers many advantages to children fortunate enough to have that opportunity. However, those who do not homeschool often utilize whatever time they do have in an effort to provide an enhanced and enriching environment in which their child can grow and learn.

How many children have access to these enriching opportunities during the school day? That greatly depends upon how many field trips are planned and executed for them. Field trips take time and effort to organize and will cost a district if busses are utilized. Some school districts severely limit the number of trips that can be scheduled in a school year.

To some, a field trip is seen as loss of learning time in the classroom and an easy day for the student and the teacher. Although it may appear to be that way, if properly planned, field trips can provide a valuable learning experience for both the student and the teacher. There should be more, not less.

Bringing experts to the classroom is another valuable learning opportunity that children typically enjoy. While just listening to someone talk about what he or she does or how something works may be interesting to some, it can also be somewhat dull. Engaging children in some kind of hands-on activity that requires them to produce a product, artifact, or visual representation will have a far greater impact on their learning.

Schools rarely tap into this unique and authentic form of learning. This is perhaps due to the inability to find willing participants who can devote some time in a classroom or maybe due to the lack of time for such a plan. It remains an underutilized option for accessing learning.

Neighborhoods have become a lost oasis in recent years with fewer and fewer resources and destinations designed for children apart from a nearby playground. Our consumer-driven society is far more interested in promoting fast foods, movie theaters, and multiple coffee shops instead of child-centered focal points. Some towns have tried to re-create that old neighborhood feel by building fashionable "wannabe" main streets complete with a Barnes & Noble, Whole Foods, and a Gap store. There may even be a fountain or clock in the center of this makeshift hometown that offers train rides or water splashes for the kiddos.

What is so unauthentic about all of this downtown deception is that people have to drive to get there, park their cars in a huge lot, and walk to the center. It is not a neighborhood, nor is it a real downtown. It's a shopping mecca padding the pockets of the big retailers.

When children can leave their home and take a reasonable walk to a bike shop, the neighborhood auto mechanic's garage, a hardware store, or the fire department, they have totally different early life experiences and discoveries than those children who don't have access to these. Likewise, children who live in a rural area often enjoy roaming expansive fields or woods, playing in a nearby creek, or building forts from their gathering of natural resources. Both are incredibly rich opportunities for learning and growth.

Some say that the world is more dangerous, and letting children of any age go anywhere without adult supervision is not wise. However, we also know that fostering independence is critical to the overall health and welfare of a child or adolescent. There is a delicate balance in this scenario, and each family determines what's best for them. However, keep in mind that freedom liberates, energizes, and builds strong foundations.

Often, the most important consideration for families with children who are determining where to live is the quality of the neighborhood school. Realtors know this quite well and bank much of their advertisements toward this end. Often schools become the hub of activity along with the local ball fields that house the various soccer, baseball, or football teams. Neighborhoods fortunate enough to have both a good school and a great ballpark are considered valuable real estate.

There are large portions of the population in the United States that find themselves in mediocre or poor schools with little or no neighborhood venues that provide a safe place for children to congregate or play. For many of these children, it seems that life has dealt them a raw deal. Their schools become a sort of sanctuary regardless of how good they are. Some students find their school a ticket to a better life, and others find it totally useless.

Often, these very schools appear to be working harder than most to provide a good education in spite of the obvious lack. Those schools who build neighborhood connections are at a greater advantage than those who don't. Families know this and so do their children.

As a society, we generally underestimate the immense potential of a neighborhood invested in children, where they learn to navigate the world outside of their homes but still within close proximity of their front porch or steps. Busy lives tend to prohibit families from seeking and sustaining strong neighborhood relationships. For the most part, there is simply not enough time in the day to nurture and build connections on that level.

Many years ago, extended families often lived near each other, providing that close-knit bond and support. That is rare today. But when it does happen, it is an amazing gift. With grandparents, aunts, uncles, and cousins nearby, a young person has a huge safety net to protect his or her comings and goings. Good neighbors can also provide that same kind of support. For those fortunate enough to have one or even two great neighbors whom they can trust and depend upon, the benefits to the children of these families are immeasurable.

Neighborhoods still hold the power to enhance the growth and learning of a child as they navigate their world. Every city planner and development committee would do well investing in their young citizens at every opportunity. Neighborhood growth and pride manifests itself in different ways. For young people, it stems from seeing themselves within the big picture. Playgrounds, ballparks, community centers, and bike, skateboard, and hiking trails all say, "You are an important part of this community, and we care about you." Small businesses that offer sports, dance, theater, arts, and other types of child-centered activities send a strong message that neighborhoods are places in which one can learn much.

Local children's service clubs, religious-affiliated activities and services, and neighborhood-sponsored events and fund-raisers are all great opportunities for young people to learn responsibility, citizenship, empathy, charity, and belonging. When they arrive in school having these types of experiences already in their repertoire, they are at a great advantage over their peers who have not. These intrinsic values and skills are not typically learned from a social studies curriculum.

Honest implementation efforts to target and value the next generation as much as possible will pay huge dividends down the road for both the city and its children. Smart neighborhoods already know this.

5

SCHOOL *DAZE*

"It is as true now as it was then that no matter what tests show, very little of what is taught in school is learned, very little of what is learned is remembered, and very little of what is remembered is used. The things we learn, remember, and use are the things we seek out or meet in the daily, serious, non-school parts of our lives."
—John Holt, *How Children Fail*

HEAVY FOG SETTLES IN

For most young people, the high school years are much more impactful than elementary or middle school, but not in the amount of knowledge amassed or remembered. It tends to be more about learning to navigate a treacherous but necessary path that will eventually lead to the prized treasures of popularity, good grades, and the right classes. For many, it provides a venue for daily gossip and laughter, which makes the whole experience worthwhile.

Quite a few adolescents dive into their classes with confidence, but with very little maturity and mediocre discipline at best. That becomes an acquired skill most of the time out of necessity. Once they discover that getting to class on time, doing the required work, and studying well enough to pass the test are a given, they usually get with the program. Even though these demands have been with them all through their schooling, they seem to forget when they reach ninth grade.

Again, those students who have been struggling all the way are not keen on this next phase of schooling as they know already what they will face. It literally becomes a make-or-break deal weighing heavily on those who have not found their niche yet. It's an ominous dark cloud hanging over a young person wherever they go. They can see and feel its presence and shudder to think how they will survive its grip.

Regardless of where students might find themselves on the Grade Point Average (GPA) spectrum, as part of the high school experience, many seek to participate in school clubs, sports, or other types of school-sponsored activities. GPA status defines who they are and is considered an entrance ticket for many activities. Maintaining a 2.0 GPA is the coveted threshold where many students find themselves hovering. While they already know that their grades determine their GPA, they still ask, "What can I do to get my GPA high enough to . . . ?" Learning is a means to an end in this case.

The need to belong and connect is evident in the many choices a young student makes on a routine basis. Because relationships are critical to the overall enjoyment of the teen years, they are entered into with caution and discernment. Tongue in cheek and obviously not a true statement, but one that sheds light on the mental reasoning that is occurring at this age. Young people are still developing discernment skills and often make bad choices because of it. These relationships have the power to ground and enhance one's development, or they can devastate and devour one's self-esteem. Reality checks occur on a regular basis at this age, and that is a good thing if the young person learns from it.

For both young men and women, this time is crucial in their overall growth and development as a person. If they believe that they are smart, popular, or "chosen," they will also believe they can rule the world. Fortunately and unfortunately, many do not see themselves in this light and will either march to their own drum or try to steal someone else's. Not many young teenagers possess the poise and confidence to speak out or stand up to their peers and wax persuasively eloquent in a different direction.

Classes offered in high school do not really provide the kind of choice students hope for or desire. Nonetheless, the required courses are part of the package and so is the overwhelming amount of homework that accompanies it. In high school, many become quite skilled at cramming for the test, pulling late nights or all-nighters in preparation for college. Not surprising, and based on some sobering statistics, many learn just enough to pass the test and retain very little moving forward.

Still, there are better-than-average crammers who survive the testing maze well enough to move on to the next grade level and courses. They memorize dates, battles, conquerors and kings, formulas, steps, and procedures. They learn to study well enough to keep themselves afloat until the next test. Those adept at memorizing are in their element in high school because much of what is required depends upon a good memory.

Teachers with over 150 students often don't ask for more than multiple-choice or very short-answer demonstrations of knowledge. Lucky for those who have learned the hunt-and-peck method. Not so good for those who learn differently.

Classroom discussions depend on how well a student has read the material or studied their notes. Most high schoolers are invited to engage in discussion more than they were in their earlier schooling years, perhaps because they are deemed capable of doing so. For certain, teenagers have opinions, and they will be heard whether invited to contribute or not.

HIGH SCHOOL: A TEAM SPORT OF WINNERS AND LOSERS

Early on in school, students are told that a C grade is average. Average is the label they assign to you when, after they've taught, you remembered just enough not to fail. It was not exactly the best place to be. But for many high schoolers, that's exactly where they find themselves. Many struggle just to hold on and not fall below the cut-off point called failure. Assignments, class participation, and tests make up the elements of these grades, and students perform juggling acts to keep them all in the air at the same time. This is a skill that schools are great at teaching.

While some manage to keep all the balls in the air, many do not. When the ball is dropped, it is typically irretrievable and chalked up to a lesson learned by way of a lower grade. In fact, the act of juggling balls becomes the core learning in most classrooms. That coupled with knowing how to get along with the teacher who adores you, doesn't really notice you, or has little tolerance for your presence. Somewhere in this mix one may find an awesome teacher who designs lessons based on students' interests, skill level, and prior experiences. When discovered, these teachers are jewels in the high school daze crown.

A bright spot for almost all students in high school is the ability to take electives. Many students in those classes wish they could stay there all day, every day. School days become bearable just knowing that these classes are available. Typically they are related to the arts, music, drama, computer programming, or innovative adventures. These are the classes that take the student to an intoxicating place described by Sir Ken Robinson as finding and being in one's element.

"Element" is a place where the things we like to do and the things we are good at come together. Sir Ken says, "We are all born with tremendous natural capacities, and . . . we lose touch with many of them as we spend time in this world. Ironically, one of the main reasons this happens is education. The result is that too many people never connect with their true talents and therefore don't know what they are really capable of achieving."[1]

With all due respect to the author, please change the word *education* to the word *school* and read the above quote again. School just doesn't deal well with connecting us to our passions. It does an excellent job, however, of restricting and directing us under the guise of getting a good education.

Many young people and their parents have discovered through all of their school years that much of what really mattered they learned outside of the school setting. The bulk of what they learned in school was how to pass the tests and then move on to the next grade level. They learned how to memorize well enough to regurgitate on demand. They learned that grades and GPA were the sum of who they are, and their life course was pretty much determined by their socioeconomic status.

They learned how to listen and comply. They also learned along the way that many schoolteachers are very caring and hardworking, sincere people who consider their profession rewarding when kids do all of the above. They don't question school policies, practices, and decades of propaganda that tell them they are better off having gone to school. In actuality, they learned that "school" is a strange experiment in compliance, coercion, and consumerism interjected with unhealthy doses of threat and humiliation working together in direct conflict with the natural way in which we all learn.

While few do, why don't more people recognize or even acknowledge this? Alfie Kohn captures this well in his book *Punished by Rewards*:

> Most things that we and the people around us do constantly . . . have come to seem so natural and inevitable that merely to pose the question, "Why are we doing this?" can strike us as perplexing—and also, perhaps, a little unsettling. On general principle, it is a good idea to challenge ourselves in this way about anything we have come to take for granted; the more habitual, the more valuable this line of inquiry.[2]

Why is it that when we ask someone to recall something they learned in school they rarely identify a specific academic learning such as a mathematical formula, or what caused Rome to fall, or the events that led up to World War I? In most cases, they'll tell you a story about an event or relational situation that was very personal and impacting. Minor academic learning becomes the sidebar.

Pondering the act of schooling, whether public, private, or religious, there are some commonalities. In my interviews with a cross section of family, friends, coworkers, and total strangers just to balance the input, the following represents their collective memories on what they remember learning in school. Comments below are verbatim.

Question: *What do you remember learning in school?*

Show up on time and how to get by with the bare minimum.

I remember learning how to write in cursive. I loved the beauty of that, although we didn't do it much. The multiplication tables had me really worried that I might never get them memorized. You guessed it. I never did.

I remember learning to memorize thousands of Latin words in grade school (if you were fairly "smart," you got to skip spelling in seventh and eighth grades and take Latin). Latin continued into high school, and I had a real gift with languages and found out that these Latin words were the basis of so many words in the English language. This mastery of Latin really helped me pass many tests in my life, even my first vocabulary test, for my first job interview.

To raise my hand before speaking.

To pledge allegiance to the flag of the USA.

I remember learning a lot of math in sixth grade. I had a math teacher who just kept giving us more challenging work, and I really enjoyed it. We used a math book that was the same textbook I was given in eleventh grade. In seventh grade, I had a different math teacher who taught the official math curriculum, and I was bored out of my mind. I don't think I ever progressed again in learning math; I just skated by on what I learned in sixth grade. About that sixth-grade teacher, I remember that she noticed me. She really noticed that I was bored in class, that I was drawing house plans, and complicated geometric art, and she asked me about what I was doing, not because she was upset or was going to punish me, but because she thought it was interesting; she thought I was interesting. When she realized I was bored, she gave me really difficult work that captured my interest. I remember being very surprised by her interest in me. Otherwise, in school I learned how to memorize, how to take tests, how to write in a way that it would be graded highly, and how to give the "right" answer. I remember giving my opinion when I was young, and learning that no one wanted to hear my opinion. I learned that it was only the teacher's opinion (or whoever was the adult or authority placed in front of me in the classroom, i.e., a book or a video or guest speaker) that mattered.

School was like a big pile of irrefutable facts, and my job was to learn all of those facts and to make sure that the teacher knew that I knew all of it. It was like that game where you look at a bunch of things, and then they take the things out of the room and you have to recall all the things you saw. The person who has the best recall wins.

I remember learning that if one is nice to the teachers and you are helpful they like you and treat you well in return.

I learned that submission to authority, conformity, and compliance are more important than critical thinking, thoughtful dialogue, and solution finding. I learned to value pop culture, consumerism, and the drive to accrue "stuff" with little regard for my (or anyone else's) mental, emotional, psychological, intellectual, and spiritual health, depth, or growth. I learned that my family and (especially) my parents could not and should not be relied upon for advice or understanding when it came to making significant life choices. These are a few of the things I learned off the top of my head. Fortunately, I have taken the long, arduous, tedious, and sometimes painful steps to UN-learn most of these things. I haven't finished yet, but I am (at least) heading in the opposite direction at this point in my life.

I learned how to cheat to get the grades I needed for college. I wasn't proud of it but couldn't deal with my parents' reaction to a C instead of an A on my report card.

I remember book reports given in front of the class and a very unfair teacher, who would not allow me to give my report on *The Good Earth* by Pearl S. Buck. First she tried saying it wasn't on the list. After I proved it was, she said, "Oh well, everybody has read that one—sit down." The whole class disagreed loudly, and she was about to give me an "E" when I remembered *Green Mansions* was on the list also. I had not read it but did see the movie with Audrey Hepburn. So I had the whole class spellbound over this story, except for Sister Z, she was still livid over the fact that I had read *The Good Earth*. So needless to say I got a C, even though I got my first standing ovation.

So I'll list all the things that come to mind academically: division (so grueling), handwriting (also grueling at first); in high school, how to write papers and vocabulary. Socially: (not by teachers, but by peers) you won't be liked if you are "different" so make yourself scarce and make sure you don't stand out, but when confronted be under the radar, while standing your ground. Through it all, be compassionate to those picked on.

My mom was very helpful in my school/home work even if it was frustrating and painful and tearful for me. Being tough in that aspect really challenged me to always do better and think for myself!

Can't really remember learning all that much except how to stay out of trouble and under the radar.

School was what everyone did every day, what choice did we have? What made it bearable was recess and PE.

MJ taught the course and made history fun and interesting. She brought the players to life. Abe and Mary were not just the sixteenth president and first lady; they were a struggling couple with a very stormy union!! We learned about affairs of the heart and that presidents were not immune to them.

In school, you do what you're told, you say what you're told, and you follow the rules. If you don't, you either get in trouble at school, or you get a poor grade, which meant getting in trouble at home.

It is all a big blur. I am sure I learned something important or I wouldn't have made it this far in life.

School was not about learning for me but more about trying to follow the rules and have fun with my friends. I dropped out from sheer boredom, grew up a few years later and taught myself with the help of a couple great mentors. I am in it now and love what I do.

I think I learned the capitals of the fifty states but I couldn't tell you today what they all are.

I learned some things early on. . . . How to read and write and do math. Most of the stuff that came after that is a fog.

In my school it was about survival, not getting beat up or bullied. Teachers turned a blind eye to what was happening. It wasn't their fault they had to teach in the toughest school in the city. Poverty, crime, drugs, racism, and hopelessness, how do you learn in that environment? You don't and the cycle repeats itself. Even with all the efforts to clean things up no one really cares about this slice of society. Some of the lucky ones make it out; most of us don't.

I heard a teacher say once, "I really didn't know what I wanted to do in life so I figured I would get a teaching degree, at least I'll have a job." That about sums up my experience in school and what I learned.

Great teachers are important in school. Without them, it is a scary place.

I learned that authority figures don't have all the answers and you have to follow your own instincts.

I learned that the ability to memorize answers to standard questions does not necessarily imply intelligence.

I learned all the basics of math and English with a little bit of history. I thought school was easy and fun but I really learned that everyone did not have a family like mine and it broadened my view of the world.

I realized authority figures could be stupid, uncaring, moronic . . . shall I go on?

As kids we were always aware that the "B" group was not the smart group. I will always remember having "A" and "B" groups. In first grade they put me in the "A" group and then a week later I was demoted to the "B" group. I knew what that meant. I wasn't that stupid, ha ha, but to be honest the "B" group had spunk and were a heck of a lot more fun!!!

MS in sixth grade (Room 203) was the other pitiful example of inhumanity gifted upon us (no doubt, to build character and to assure me that, in God's justice, there would be at least one demon to torment me in Hell).

I had a selfish wish to be mentored. I yearned for a teacher to recognize some "talent" or some "gift" in me that I could develop. I wanted to break free of the blue-collar background and feel better about myself. This did not happen. There was little opportunity for those of us who could not stay after school to work on extra committees or projects and "to shine." I feel every student should have the opportunity to discover their strengths, but school systems then and school systems now still benefit and single out those who have the most opportunity—money, access, motivation, and intelligence.

Although these comments represent a random sampling of respondents, they accurately capture the essence of what factory schooling does and does not provide. This is a sad commentary on the state of education in our country. In a future chapter, current students will weigh in on their experiences. The comparisons are uncanny. In the meantime, what can we take away from this list? What do you remember learning in school?

6

SCHOOLS OF EDUCATION

"If you don't know where you're going any road can take you there."
—Lewis Carroll, *Alice's Adventures in Wonderland*

THE PATH OF GOOD INTENTIONS

Those who desire to support the learning of another often choose teaching as a career. For young people, the call to teach often comes at a high cost, because it is not the best paying profession, nor is it easy. Over the years, fewer students are choosing that path, which in many areas has created a teacher shortage. Low pay, along with a high rate of teacher burnout, causes some to rethink this career altogether.

In the schools of education on university campuses, the requisite humanities courses are scheduled each semester and are usually delivered via a lecture and regurgitate format. There are still multiple-choice exams, but they have become much more devious than the ones in the K–12 system. They are seen by some as a plot to weed out those who are really listening and reading their books from those who are just guessing. Choices are not so clear between a, b, c, d, both a and b, both b and c, or none of the above. Talk about confusing! And where is the learning in all this except how to better understand the hunt-and-peck method.

Some classes ask for written essays to demonstrate one's knowledge of the material heard in the lecture, which works well for those who can maneuver with language. In this format, one never knows exactly what the professor is looking for even though all of the correct information was given and explained. Mysterious questions or comments appear on the sides of assignments and tests with no indication of where the thought had come from or why it was important. It is best described as a mind game and considered normal practice in the higher education arena.

After a couple of years of mandated classes for education majors, students may be able to take a few electives. In the case of college rigor, these are often seen as an easy A to boost one's overall Grade Point Average (GPA). Again, for the most part, students learn to navigate the college conundrum. If they haven't dropped out by year two, there is a good chance that they will make it through all four or, in many cases, five and six.

Within teacher preparation courses, one typically finds volumes of pedagogy, various viewpoints on educational philosophies, several developmental and educational psychology theories, and tons of research. There also may be specific course content required for those teaching middle school or high school subjects.

Usually a token special education class is thrown in the mix and counted toward the overall educational requirement, except for those who have chosen to teach students with disabilities. Their course work will involve a few additional requirements in an attempt to prepare them to teach a more individualized program. For the most part, courses in grading and test development are nonexistent.

The basics in any college or university education training come by way of lesson planning, delivery, and reflection. Once content is mastered from taking the required courses, the next step is to combine that knowledge with the art of lesson planning. Lessons are usually scripted at first to provide the student examples in which to construct their own lesson. The infamous Bloom's Taxonomy[1] and Maslow's Hierarchy of Needs[2] are the foundations of most teacher preparation programs. Although over the years various versions of these mainstays have been introduced.

As teacher hopefuls gather all the foundational theory and skills, they typically develop and then present lessons in front of peers and professors. They are usually offered feedback and constructive criticism. Lesson rewrites are encouraged and recognized as good practice.

In the midst of lesson design and delivery, other important skills come to the forefront. Soon-to-be teachers study various strategies that promise to keep students attentive and engaged. These are often found in more current readings from school reformers or researchers who have done studies at actual schools where these strategies have been used. Teachers willingly gather as many ideas as possible to arm themselves for the final test—a real classroom.

Over the years, universities and colleges that offer teacher training and certification do so within the system's current structural mold. Teachers are prepped to teach in the school systems that follow, for the most part, the prescribed format for teaching. Direct, didactic instruction sprinkled with a few innovative or hands-on ideas, and seasoned with strong classroom management, are coveted skills that almost guarantee employment. Classroom control is at the top of every supervising professor's must-see list when visiting the student teacher.

Far less time is actually spent in a classroom than what is generally desired on the part of the college student. A brief stint as a student teacher allows for a "see and feel" experience but not one that enables the student to fully experience and demonstrate the art of teaching. Once teachers have made the grade and passed with a degree, they begin the task of locating suitable employment. Graduated and newly dubbed classroom teachers start the interview process hoping to land the perfect job that will help pay their rent and, in many cases, their college loans.

Once hired, they are usually given a performance evaluation that will determine whether they will be asked to stay beyond the first two years. This is known as tenure and has been the topic of debate for many who see this time as too short to make a solid determination of the teacher's skill level and effectiveness. Teachers rarely see that time as too short. For most, it can't end soon enough as they have to be on their toes, so to speak, the entire time.

Depending upon the state in which they live, new teachers may be offered a mentor or a coach. These mentors and coaches are usually teachers themselves who have earned the right to this distinction on the basis of their effectiveness in the classroom and rapport with students.

Two years of continuous coaching and targeted professional development seals the deal for most teachers with regard to tenure. Once under tenure, teachers can't be dismissed so easily. Most teachers don't have to worry about that possibility, because they appear to abide by the rules set forth by the school and district. More important, almost all teachers want to do well.

Many teachers continue to earn professional credit by way of course work, advanced degrees, and extended professional development. Having done so, they are offered advancement on their salary schedule when credit is earned and required paperwork is filed. Some teachers never avail themselves to continuing education while others sign up for course work long after earning a master's degree or advanced certification. In some cases, teachers may even pursue a doctoral program or a national certification, both very rigorous processes.

In any event, there are some teachers who are lifelong learners and others who are not so inclined. This is rather intriguing to those on the outside looking into the world of teaching. As in any service-oriented profession, learning as much as you can to assist those whom you serve is seen as necessary and critical. Think of doctors, nurses, car mechanics, or air traffic controllers. If they rested on the skills they learned when they were first trained or hired, they would be way behind the times. New technology, infrastructure, scientific discoveries, and refuted practices all help to better inform them in their current practices.

As a general rule of thumb, teachers, and more often school systems themselves, cringe at the thought of the latest and greatest. They see it more as the same old package just recycled under a different name. And in many cases, that is an accurate description. Districts may spend hours, money, and materials bringing new ideas to the teaching staff only to find them resistant and, in some cases, even hostile. That is not surprising since there is often a failure to ask the teachers what they need or want to learn about in order to grow professionally.

Another interesting dynamic occurs when teachers view this additional learning as the school system's responsibility, not theirs. Many insist that if new information is needed and required to do their jobs, then the school system should pay for it, whereas, in most cases, the school system sees teacher professional development as a co-responsibility. Offering teachers training during the school day and paying for their time to participate in professional development after school hours is one way that is accomplished.

ENTER THE UNION

Teacher unions have the potential to become a breeding ground for disgruntled employees who see the system as the enemy out to get them at every turn. Their existence is seen by some as necessary to keep the management in line and in touch with their demands. Frequently those who belong to unions are passionate about children and learning. They are also willing and open to dialogue that promotes shared and common agreements.

Occasionally there are those union representatives and members who have another type of agenda, and this becomes painfully clear as they begin to speak. It doesn't take long to learn that their agenda is not about children at all. It's about them. They shroud their comments in the philosophy of "what's good for me is good for my students." In some cases, this may be true; oftentimes, it is a ploy to get greater autonomy, less accountability, and an increased paycheck.

Teaching as a profession is not about real autonomy because the system is obliged to control and direct what happens in the classroom. It's their job. Likewise, teaching will always have some kind of accountability attached to it. Our clients, the parents and community, demand this. In addition, the bestowers of funding, both state and federal, mandate it. The system is working just as it was designed to, and thinking that it can function in any other way is a futile and unrealistic notion. Schools are working as they were planned to. Nothing new here.

However, from a teacher's perspective, they are asked to stand and deliver every day. They are asked to maintain control of more than thirty to forty students, providing specific attention to those with special and diverse needs, and to ensure that the entire curriculum is covered by the end of the school year. They are charged with keeping large masses of students in order, knowing when a child is struggling, offering individual assistance, and developing engaging lessons.

They are directed to contact home, compute and maintain grades, manage accounts, and monitor health issues. They are guided to reflect on their practice, make necessary adjustments or improvements, and adhere to identified policy and imposed deadlines. They are expected to do all of this with a positive can-do attitude and smiles on their faces. Many do just that.

Some say this is no different from any other demanding professional job. Others might see this as a recipe doomed to failure or chance at the very least. Teachers are incredibly brave people. They are often fearless in the face of extraordinary daily demands. Many of them pour their hearts into teaching and simply love what they do. They are willing to learn and apply new strategies and observe masters at work. Teaching is an art, not a science, and given the proper tools and enough time each artist creates his or her own unique masterpiece. These masterpieces are evidenced in the learning that takes place in their classrooms.

However, there are flaws within this schooling system that if fixed could easily remedy much of what is problematic. Brave visionaries have attempted to chip away at the iceberg but not without a grueling trial-and-error process. Real change is daunting, exhausting, and very messy work.

Many still do not believe that there is a real need for substantive change on the foundational level. There is little conversation on the subject. However, when districts, schools, teachers, and administrators come together with families, students, and other stakeholders to discuss and plan what they collectively deem important and vital for the educational well-being of their students, great things can happen. Keep that in mind as we proceed.

CAN ANYONE ANSWER THESE QUESTIONS?

The following are a few questions that some have pondered over the years. It appears that very few in the "schooling" world are able to adequately and intelligently respond to them. Typically, the responses involve a litany of excuses, and lack of courage and conviction to confront the brutal reality. What is most disheartening is a certain arrogance and sometimes apathy that shifts blame to parents, lack of resources, or the students themselves as if they are the root of the problem.

- How does the act of sending young people off to a school where they stay confined for six or seven hours, mostly in the same room with the same teacher, create the optimal conditions for learning, and why are we still doing that?

- Why do we force children into a one-size-fits-all model, and when we determine that they don't fit, label them academically at risk or behavior problems?
- Why are we so convinced that report cards in the way of letter or number grades are an effective way to determine whether learning has taken place?
- Why ten months of school and two months off in the summer?
- Why do we cram so much information into those ten months and then identify students who need more time to learn as failures who must repeat the same experience with the hope of getting different results? And why do teachers have to spend almost the whole first month of school reviewing what was supposed to be "learned" the year before?
- Why do we think that the way we prepare teachers in our universities really prepares them for the current realities of our schools?
- How can teachers effectively meet the individual needs of each learner with twenty-five to thirty-five students in a classroom?
- How can we justify not meeting the individual needs of each learner because there are twenty-five to thirty students in the classroom?
- Why is it that children are born curious and we kill that off in about third or fourth grade with drill-and-kill activities?
- Why have years of reform and funding not given us the desired, sustainable results, and why do we still have children of poverty and color underperforming at alarming rates?
- Why is it that 32 percent of all suspended students are black, and why are black students twice as likely as whites to be suspended or expelled?
- Why do only 22 percent of black males who begin at a four-year college graduate within six years?
- Why do blacks compose only 3.2 percent of lawyers, 3 percent of doctors, and less than 1 percent of architects in this country?
- Why are more and more parents opting to provide their children with alternative forms of schooling, such as Montessori, parent-created charters, homeschooling, un-schooling, and online learning options?

- Why do we continue to force children to attend public schooling and label parents who choose other viable options as fanatics, incapable, elitist, or radical?
- Why do we spend millions upon millions of dollars on error-ridden publisher textbooks and instructional materials?
- Why do we build multimillion-dollar school facilities with classrooms that resemble anything but authentic learning environments?
- Why are so many people writing books and articles on how schools failed them?
- Why are we so satisfied with the continued practice of systematically disenfranchising young people of color or poverty by forcing them to accept the "school myth" that says follow the rules, listen and learn, and you can be somebody?
- Why do we allow some teachers to continue working with our children when we know they are ineffective? How can we justify this practice, and why aren't more parents outraged?
- Why do we restrict learning to a classroom and teaching to a degree from a university?
- Why do parents request certain teachers and not others?
- When will the system change, and how long do we have to wait?
- When do we listen to the voice of the child?

THE PROBLEM OF EDUCATIONAL MALPRACTICE

These are valid questions that deserve answers. When there are so many questions shrouding the topic of schooling, why do we not ask these questions more often and demand answers? It seems that unless school change is legislated, nothing substantially different ever happens. Schools are on a powerless and perpetual "lockdown," not able to move about freely or think far enough out of the box to make any inroads that lead to real learning.

We hear about newly created schools that have tried innovative and creative ways to approach the act of learning and have found positive results for students. There are actually quite a few that have emerged recently. Many of these are based on democratic principles where students have vested interest and input into their education. The current schooling system as we know it doesn't really allow this kind of radical departure from the norm and actually frowns upon any such efforts as renegade and risky. The underlying and root concern is that any kind of substantive innovation may render the schools themselves useless. Do we really need a place called school in order to learn?

There are many who believe that the collection and distribution of public taxes will provide what is needed in our public schools. At least, that was the original intent. There are still those who believe that by pouring more money into Pre-K through 12 schooling, we will see equity, access, and achievement for all. There is a strongly held notion that unless we do this, nothing will substantially change and the system will continue to fail our children in spite of our grand efforts.

Another serious and often minimized contributing factor to the problems within our schools is the ingrained racism in our country that still "oppresses" those of color and low socioeconomic status. Don't be fooled thinking that racism or classism has been eradicated in the world of schooling because we have become an enlightened, twenty-first-century people. The playing field is not fully level unless every adult in every school is culturally proficient. They aren't.

Cultural proficiency, as defined by Randall Lindsey, is the "honoring of differences among cultures, viewing diversity as a benefit, and interacting knowledgeably and respectfully among a variety of cultural groups."[3] Through the work of Randy and his team, they have observed that "schools begin to change when their leaders recognize the disparities that exist in our schools and then intentionally raise issues of bias, preferences, legitimization, privilege, and equity. By choosing to face these issues and grapple with them directly to understand their effects on student learning, these leaders are moving their schools and districts towards cultural proficient practices."[4]

There is not one simple solution to this gigantic problem that has grown exponentially over the years. Many books, speakers, articles, and research point to isolated results and possible causes of our failure to "educate" our children. There are well-respected men and women who try to tackle this issue from every conceivable perspective. Rarely does anyone "touch" the sacred cow—which is the act of schooling itself. School is a given in our society, and therefore we must deal with it, or work to educate in spite of it.

7

LEADERSHIP LESSONS

"Institutions like the American schooling system have a hierarchy that maintains and runs the system. The hierarchy's job is to manage the system, and in the case of the institution of school, the people being managed by the system—the students—are being processed for eventual inclusion into every other institution in society. This is good for the institutions and the managers but a tragedy for the little humans being processed." —Jason Laird

ONWARD AND UPWARD

Leading a school or school system is both rewarding and challenging. It's rewarding because of the positive effect it can have on student and adult learning. Because learning is such a unique and different experience for each individual, leading those in one's charge toward that end can also be quite challenging. Getting everyone on the same page when it comes to values, beliefs, and expectations for student learning is nearly impossible.

Teachers who do well in the classroom and exhibit school leadership are often encouraged to move on to pursue administrative certification. Those who take an administrative path are required to meet various state requirements in order to achieve that status. Once finished with these requirements, they are officially deemed an administrator with a credential to prove it.

Within the schooling system, there is an obvious pecking order that usually means first fulfilling the role of an assistant principal, then principal, and if desired a district-level administrative position. Some are in their niche as school leaders, and others find great satisfaction leading in a broader capacity. Whatever leadership role is decided, it brings heavy responsibility and requires large amounts of patience.

Leading school teams to become functional, intentional, and focused on the needs of the students rather than the adults is a challenging endeavor. It is challenging because people generally don't like change. The process of facilitating change can be invigorating, and at the same time, exhausting. To do it successfully takes specific and learned skills that most administrative credential programs do not cover in depth. Apart from a cursory read or discussion on adult learning or change theory, the intensity and skill it takes to facilitate substantive change is left untouched and unfamiliar to many aspiring leaders.

Even in schools and systems where child-centered practices appear to guide staff, there is always a need to improve the quality of that endeavor. While the efforts of teaching staff may be noble, there are many ingrained practices that are just not effective. Schools spin their wheels trying to figure out what to do looking for some kind of remedy to help those children who are not faring well. They rarely focus on the basic structure and processes that often work in complete contrast to how one learns best.

Eager to do well, newly appointed leaders learn as much as they can about the culture and values of their community. Most often they do this by meeting and getting to know all of the players. They work to build relationships and then set out to create optimal learning conditions. They want their school to be a place where parents and children are welcome and happy. They may find a group of teachers and staff already working together to deliver what they perceive as a top-quality educational program for their students.

Most administrators dive into a new position ready to work hard and roll up their sleeves. However, most encounter mountains almost instantly in the form of traditions, practices, and firmly held territory carved out by more than a few well-meaning but nonbudging individuals. This is new administrator boot camp, and it can be grueling. A lofty goal of a fast- and forward-moving agenda may come to a screeching halt with an inevitable large dose of reality.

Cycles and downturns in the national economy affect our schools. With dwindling resources, both budget and people, priorities shift out of necessity. Often, just keeping the boat afloat becomes the goal. Even though there may be many areas needing attention, they will have to wait, or at best, maintain current status until the clouds dissipate at some unknown point in time. This can be very frustrating and disappointing as important programs may be set aside. This is the direct result of having to prioritize funding, or the proverbial robbing Peter to pay Paul.

Program efforts in visual and performing arts, music, physical education, and enrichment are often found sitting on the back burner or nonexistent in many elementary schools across the country. Band-Aid approaches are applied to these areas while more of our attention, time, and energy is shifted to satisfy ever-increasing federal mandates. In spite of fluctuating funding and a plethora of unknowns, good leaders march on with strong resolve and determination to provide what they believe is a quality educational experience for their students. Institutionalized wisdom dictates the script and those in the trenches often believe it.

Observing firmly rooted practices from a district administration perch, intuitive and savvy leaders come to realize that much of what they are required to do makes little to no sense. The rules and education codes are thick and unyielding. Unnecessary "hoops" of both state and federal mandates become increasingly cumbersome with mounds of required documentation and reporting.

In order to tackle and manage all of these strongholds, district or central office management becomes a necessary component, not to mention clerical and administrative assistance to handle the volume of work generated by such mandates. The larger the district, the more help is needed.

WHAT ARE WE DOING, PEOPLE?

We are a country of mega-institutions and mega-mandates, laws, and bureaucratic red tape. This is quite evident in the institution of school. We have become so accustomed to this leaching octopus that we don't even notice it sucking the life out of real and meaningful educational opportunities. We have lost our moral compass regarding our most precious gifts, our children.

First, we force children to attend school and tell parents that we know how to educate their young ones better than they do by virtue of our diplomas, degrees, and experience. We snatch them up at a very young age and then proceed to systematically push them through the maze of schooling knowing full well that we will lose some along the way. Apparently that doesn't matter. Some of these "missing in action" young ones check out long before they officially drop out of school. They have lost interest, motivation, and purpose.

Second, we convince everyone that schools work for most children because if they pay attention and study they will earn good grades, go on to college, graduate, and become successful, contributing adults. This is not even true, especially when you measure learning using the current system of teach it and test it. What has been known for a very long time, but is slow to take root in the world of schooling, is that *there is no precise measure of human learning*.

Third, we train students to listen as we talk, memorize for recall, take notes for studying, and accurately spit out what we've told them on a test. This is not real learning. This is regurgitation on command. Learning is not the result of teaching. Children learn in different ways at different times in different circumstances.

One size does not and never will fit all. Each person is unique and each learns in his or her own way. Many learn by doing, by experimenting, and by trial and error. Many learn by watching a master or practicing under a master. Many can teach themselves contrary to what skeptics say.

Finally, we perpetuate the notion that there is really nothing wrong with the way we are schooling children today. In fact, we hold ourselves in high regard acknowledging our accomplishments and noting our successes. We measure how well we have done using a self-designed construct that is imprecise and irrelevant. Test scores, school and teacher popularity scores, and a safe school campus all earn us the right to distinction. Again, institutionalized wisdom propagates this belief.

All that can change when something goes wrong. Something like an active shooter or intruder on campus, or a teacher having inappropriate contact with a student. Something like dismal test scores after teaching the new and not-so-impressive common core standards that claim rigor and relevance. There are a plethora of scenarios that can turn a school's image upside down.

CHOICE: THE NASTY WORD IN PUBLIC SCHOOLS

As one might expect, in the eyes of the institutional public schooling world, homeschooling has been frowned upon for many years as an inferior option for children. Parents whose state affords them this right must prove their curriculum and progress in order to implement this option. Parents give many different reasons for homeschooling their children.

In 2007, the most common reason parents gave as the most important was a desire to "provide religious or moral instruction" (36 percent of parents). This reason was followed by a concern "about school environment" (such as safety, drugs, or negative peer pressure) (21 percent); "dissatisfaction with academic instruction" (17 percent); and "other reasons," including family time, finances, travel, and distance (14 percent). Parents of about 7 percent of homeschooled students cited the desire to provide their child with a nontraditional approach to education as the most important reason for homeschooling, and the parents of another 6 percent of students cited a child's health problems or special needs.[1]

A recent *Huffington Post* article reported that more than two million U.S. students in grades K–12 were homeschooled in 2010, accounting for nearly 4 percent of all school-aged children, according to the National Home Education Research Institute. Studies suggest that those who go on to college will outperform their peers. Students coming from a home school graduated college at a higher rate than their peers—66.7 percent compared to 57.5 percent—and earned higher grade point averages along the way, according to a study that compared students at one doctoral university from 2004 to 2009.[2]

> "They're also better socialized than most high school students," says Joe Kelly, an author and parenting expert who home-schooled his twin daughters. "I know that sounds counterintuitive because they're not around dozens or hundreds of other kids every day, but I would argue that's why they're better socialized," Kelly says. "Many homeschoolers play on athletic teams, but they're also interactive with

students of different ages. Home-schooled students often spend less time in class," Kelly says, "giving them more opportunity to get out into the world and engage with adults and teens alike. The socialization thing is really a nonissue for most home-schoolers," he says. "They're getting a lot of it."[3]

In the same June 2012 *Huffington Post* article, written by Kelsey Sheehy, Jesse Orlowski, homeschooled from the age of three and an eighteen-year-old San Diego native, shared his experience:

> The flexibility of home schooling allowed him to focus on his passions: math and science. As a junior, Orlowski convinced a physics professor at San Diego State University to let him sit in on an upper-level electrodynamics class. He later helped that professor with research projects. "I can go out and say, 'OK, what class do I want to take, from what professor, at what college in San Diego?' and then I just go out and try and contact them," he says. "Most people would be skeptical at first and then I'd meet with them and they'd say, 'Alright, let's give this a try.'"[4]

The article continued:

> Orlowski enlisted the help of admissions counselor and author Marjorie Hansen Shaevitz, who previously worked in the office of the dean of students at Stanford University, to help craft his home-schooling experience into a high school transcript. Home-schooled students often choose academic and social pursuits because they find them important and meaningful, and college admissions officers are drawn to that authenticity, Shaevitz says.
>
> "They have to take account of time that other students have structured," she says. "The possibilities of showing all the kinds of things that colleges are looking for—curiosity, confidence, resourcefulness, ability to deal with challenges—you name it. That's a part of being a home-schooled student."
>
> Rather than a hindrance, home-schooling was an asset, Orlowski says, one that landed him acceptance into 10 top-tier schools, including Princeton University, Vanderbilt University, and the Massachusetts Institute of Technology. Orlowski will attend MIT in the fall and plans a double major in math and physics.[5]

While this is only one example of many and a homeschooling success story, it does underscore the limitless possibilities that homeschooling affords. More and more families are choosing this option as a viable alternative. However, information gathered from the U.S. Department of Education, National Center for Education Statistics (2009) indicates that more white students were homeschooled than black or Hispanic students or students from other racial/ethnic groups, and white students constituted the majority of homeschooled students (77 percent).[6]

White students (3.9 percent) had a higher homeschooling rate than blacks (0.8 percent) and Hispanics (1.5 percent), but were not measurably different from students from other racial/ethnic groups (3.4 percent). Students in two-parent households made up 89 percent of the homeschooled population, and those in two-parent households with one parent in the labor force made up 54 percent of the homeschooled population. The latter group of students had a higher homeschooling rate than their peers: 7 percent, compared with 1 to 2 percent of students in other family circumstances. In 2007, students in households earning between $25,001 and $75,000 per year had higher rates of homeschooling than their peers from families earning $25,000 or less a year.[7]

These statistics tell a very interesting story, and one that should not be surprising. Poor families and those having only one parent present will be less likely to homeschool and more likely to need the public school option. While there are some innovative and child-centered public schools, few are available to many of the inner-city poor families.

The movie *Waiting for Superman* told this tale as it surfaced the plight of families stuck in underperforming schools. While charter schools were offered up as an olive branch of hope, not all charter schools are created equally. There is no level playing field for those students who cannot rely upon their own parents to homeschool or send them to a private school or win the lottery for an innovative and effective charter school. They are stuck and oppressed in this so-called free schooling. It is not free when it holds young minds captive in a mediocre existence. We can do better.

All over the country and in many school districts, the *schooling machine* continues to function much in the same way it has for decades. It churns out so-called educated young people ready for the world ahead of them. The real education, however, actually starts when the young person is confronted with what comes next. In many cases, he or she doesn't have a clue exactly how to get there.

Repeating basic college courses two or more times has become the norm. What used to take four years to complete now takes five or six years. Not all college students fall into this category; however, for an alarming many this is a reality.

A recent *Washington Post* article reported that "graduating college is taking longer and isn't cheap. It costs $15,933 more in tuition, fees and room and board for every extra year in a public two-year college and $22,826 for every added year in a public four-year college, according to a new report by the nonprofit Complete College America."[8]

A recent Education Department study found that students take 20.3 more credits for the average amount of courses they fail. The article goes on to say that "50 out of the more than 580 public four-year institutions report on-time graduation rates at or above 50 percent their first time."[9]

The real issue is that we (schools) have systematically disenfranchised a ton of young people. Some of these are more obvious than others, but in general, students of color, males, females, gifted, challenged, poor, and those we call "average" are frequently dealt a raw deal. So who is left in this classroom?

It is rather sad that we have come to expect and depend upon schools to be just the way they are, and when any kind of substantive, commonsense change is proposed it might as well be an Armageddon proposal. What do we fear, and why are we not willing to have an open and honest dialogue about the way we do school?

At some point in this cacophony of thought, the voices and faces of all the young children we are robbing of a rich and liberating education come to the forefront of our minds and silence is no longer justified. These children deserve more from us collectively. It is time for action.

If you believe that there is nothing in need of change with the way we currently do school, then you can save yourself time and stop here. There will be many who doubt that the kind of change suggested in the remaining chapters of this book is even doable, let alone worthwhile. However, if we are open and honest, we might just find the will to tackle this much-needed change.

8

EXPOSING THE TRUTH

"If we are to deliver transformative improvement, it is not enough to wedge new practices into familiar schools and districts; we must re-imagine the system itself." —Frederick M. Hess, *Education Unbound*

A REPEATED CYCLE OF ABUSE

There are those who are strong and outspoken supporters of public education, believing that whatever obstacles or challenges we face can be overcome with determination, commitment, and proper funding. Ideologically, that is indeed true. However, many of these same advocates avail themselves to alternatives when it comes to sending their own child to their local public school. Perhaps locating and attending a thriving, innovative, and relevant public school depends upon one's zip code.

The federal government, desperate for seeking out those "model" public school practices across the country, recently launched what it called the "Ready for Success 2015 Back-to-School Bus Tour." Department of Education head Arne Duncan spent time observing classrooms, participating in roundtable discussions with students contemplating college, and highlighting all the great happenings across seven states. He also made stops at reputable and innovative universities such as Carnegie Mellon in Pittsburgh, Pennsylvania.[1]

It doesn't take a university degree to understand that this launch was pure propaganda and a costly attempt at damage control. This publicity blitz was not a credible response to our ongoing and systematic disenfranchising of children and young people every day in our schools. This happens at different times and in different ways. It is often a direct result of remediation courses, summer school, failing a grade, low expectations and tracking, multiple interventions, longer school days, hours of homework, unfair grading practices, a plethora of tests, and little to no freedom of choice.

The intent of this bus tour was to take the focus off of what is not working and to send a message to America that it may not be as bad as we think. Although the Department of Education did not choose to interview all the students we are failing to serve, it certainly would have provided a much clearer picture of the severity of this problem and the casualties along the way. Why are those voices not in the mix on this extravagant bus tour? Why aren't all schools places where children can thrive and succeed?

It is intensely disturbing to find that well-meaning public school advocates refuse to hear the voices of those students who tell us that school did not work for them—those students who say school is boring, out of touch with reality, unyielding, and overcontrolling. It is heartbreaking to observe the willing abdication of parent responsibility regarding the education of their children. Instead, it is handed over to legislators, textbook publishers, and those with agenda-driven purse strings.

Children in need are most often provided inferior and unacceptable educational options. In a country where the premise of public education is supposedly built on the underlying principles of liberty and justice for all, our schools are the antithesis of that bedrock belief. In fact, there is no freedom, no real choice, and no room for deviation. Conformity, compliance, and compulsion are the mainstay, and all in the name of free education for the masses.

Our current school systems are not free; the costs are staggering on many levels, the most important being the way we have systematically oppressed millions of children with a one-size-fits-all approach.

It is alarming and inhumane that children are herded through our school system like cattle, prodded if they veer off to the left or right and forced into a contrived learning environment, one that must be controlled due to sheer numbers. The majority of teachers mean no harm and truly love children and learning. They simply have been taught only one method—how to control, how to keep order, and how to command attention.

They have been trained to cover material and how to follow curriculum so it lasts about nine months. They have been taught to stand and deliver and that children won't learn if we don't put grades on student work. They are told to differentiate for thirty or more students at the same time and given strategies for keeping kids "busy" in order to accomplish this monumental feat. They are taught to teach what will be assessed on the high-stakes test and are judged on how well they do this in the given time frame.

So that is the model—that is how it all gets done. This model is deeply rooted in our schools and is rarely questioned. Most of us were schooled in this model and so were our children. If a child makes it through this system and does fairly well according to grades that are given, we deem them and the system successful. If they don't do well, the *student* is considered a failure, not the system.

The slogan that says, "All students will learn" is noteworthy and in some cases encouragingly proven given the thoughtful and child-centered practices one might observe. However, this is the exception—not the norm.

Our students are products of what we model. Teach them dependence and submission and they comply. Teach them that certain behaviors trigger rewards and they catch on to the cues. Teach them to sit and raise hands and speak only when spoken to and they acquiesce over time. Teach them that passing the test and getting good grades is the sum of their existence in school and they work toward that end having no comprehension of what real, deep, lasting learning is.

Teach them to find the correct answer, and they never strive, struggle, or persist at something difficult. They search for the quickest and easiest way out in order to meet the ultimate goal of producing the right answer. These seem to be conditions ripe for promulgating the art of cheating, copying, and manipulating the system—methods that are unknowingly facilitated.

Fostering intrinsic motivation and encouraging curiosity in our students is not taught in most college and university education courses and is definitely not on the radar at most teacher in-service or professional development offerings. When it is mentioned, it is laughed off as out of touch with reality.

Alfie Kohn is a credible voice who repeatedly calls on the schooling community to rethink what they are doing. His work should be a must-read alongside teacher preparation materials or teacher in-service learning opportunities. It is simply too important to neglect and far too costly to ignore. Motivation and curiosity are lost in the factory school model of education.

Suspensions and expulsions are another important indicator that schools are not working for many of our students. Here are some sobering statistics. In the state of Maryland, in the 2012–2013 school year, there were 92,215 students suspended or expelled, with an alarming disproportionate percentage of those being students of color.[2]

In California (2013–2014), the number was one in every twenty students suspended and one in every thousand students expelled. There were 366,629 students suspended and 9,553 students expelled in California that year.[3]

Truancy rates across the country are also of great concern. The truancy rate for California for the 2013–2014 school year was at 31.14 percent. According to the Data Quest website accessed via the California Department of Education, 1,995,672 truancy incidents were reported out of a total of 6,236,672 students at the time of the statewide census enrollment data collection.[4] This is alarming data.

Why don't students come to school? There are many reasons, none of which are easily remedied. The blame game usually begins with the school sending threatening notices home to the parents or caregivers reminding them of the compulsory attendance law. Often students are reprimanded for laziness, lack of responsibility, and even disrespect. However, there is one glaringly obvious factor that few ever address or consider—the way we are "schooling" them.

The truant will tell you when you ask. They cite boredom, irrelevancy, no purpose, already failing so why bother, and a list of other reasons that we brush off as excuses. In fact, some of these may be the very reason that they risk truancy. They receive no real benefit from attending school. They see no value in what they are learning or how it relates to their world. No one in school is able to provide them with a reasonable answer or motivation for coming. So, they don't come or they find other ways to access their education.

There are other factors that impact classroom learning. Students who are inquisitive or seeking to interact with their learning environment are often labeled as "problems" and sometimes even medicated. Teachers recommend to parents that they have their children tested for ADHD, autism, oppositional defiance disorder, or various other conditions of late. This is mainly so that the teacher can teach and the other students in the class can learn without interruption. Parents are torn between what they perceive and what the school is telling them.

Some parents have already sought medical advice themselves as they grapple with how best to handle their very active children. Why are so many children being diagnosed and medicated? Is there truly an epidemic of extremely active children? Where were these children in the 1950s, 1960s, or later? Will this perceived epidemic worsen over time? How many children will need to be medicated or bribed just to stay in school?

Jerry Mintz, in his article "The Ten Signs You Need to Find a Different Kind of Education for Your Child," weighs in on this topic with laser-like clarity:

> Be wary of these diagnoses and keep in mind that much of the traditional school curriculum these days is behavior control. If test requirements limit a teacher's ability to engage students, if students are discouraged from following their own passions and expected to sit for five or six hours a day with limited personal attention and interaction, I suggest it's the school that has the disease, EDD— Educational Deficit Disorder—and it might be time to get your child out of that situation![5]

There is much to learn outside of the traditional classroom that cannot be replicated there. Trying to keep children contained in one room for six or more hours with few breaks and little to no authentic access to the world around them is wrong. For a very active child this amounts to hostage-taking and imprisonment. Yet, this is what we do every day in our efforts to meet the needs of *all* children.

In school, there is little room for deviation or gross motor development apart from physical education or short recesses. Instead, students are instructed to sit quietly and pay attention to the auditory signals for twelve long years. A square peg is flat out of luck in this scenario because it will never fit into the proverbial round hole. After a few tries to fit in, it will either muddle through, losing any hope of gaining momentum, or it will give up altogether and quit. This inability to fit the mold manifests itself in truancy, disruption, and apathy. On a sad note, this usually happens by third grade—at eight or nine years old.

What good comes from the conditioned response method? How does that impact learning? Why do we insist on doing it this way when we know it doesn't work for a vast majority of students? Why are we willing to repeatedly watch this happen? These questions deserve an honest answer.

John Holt was a true pioneer in out-of-the-box schooling. In his 1976 book titled *Instead of Education*, he provides compelling arguments against compulsory schooling. While some saw this as radical ideology at that time, we now see an urgent shift happening with regard to his premise of educational freedom and choice. More and more parents and students are opting for different ways to learn apart from the regular classroom scenario. There are multitudes of options for learning that one can access. Why not access and utilize these options for credit as opposed to the forced bottom-in-seat method.

Seat time is so contrived and never amounts to the same kind of authentic learning that we know can happen in a variety of venues. Our children are crying out for something better, and we hold on to the old paradigm.

John Holt sums it up quite well in this particular quote from his book *Instead of Education*:

> As long as schools remain compulsory, coercive, and competitive— any changes we make in them will not go very deep or very far or last for very long. Those who talk of reforming schools seem like people trying to bail the water out of a boat with a big hole in the bottom. A case might be made that we have to keep bailing until we can get to a place where we can fix the hole. But the reformers don't seem to know that there is a hole.[6]

In summary, educators have done their jobs well—exactly the way they were taught. Children and parents honor us for it. There is a badge of honor one receives having survived the force-fed method of learning. It is called a diploma. It may or may not have much value depending upon what comes after the senior year in high school. Based on the multitudes of young people who spend far longer than two years in local community colleges trying to "catch up" to an acceptable level of performance, the diploma means very little.

There is also an honor conferred upon teachers having produced well-educated young people. "Teacher Appreciation Day" has turned into a week and, in some cases, a whole month. Typically recognizing and thanking teachers for a job well done is appropriate. Teaching is a noble endeavor and a wonderful opportunity to guide and facilitate learning and growth in young people.

Teachers know, however, that not all of their students meet the required mark. If given the opportunity, most teachers would have utilized all the time and means necessary to ensure every student's success. However, grade levels, bell schedules, tracking, and high-stakes test preparation prohibit that opportunity. This is indeed very sad. We need to rethink what we are doing.

In order to truly meet the learning needs of all children, the system has to hear their voices and learn from what they tell us.

9

VOICES FROM THE FIELD

"The real way to learn anything is to go out and experience it and let your curiosity lead you." —Ted, the Man in the Yellow Hat, *Curious George*, by Margret and H. A. Rey

IT'S TIME TO LISTEN

Children are adept at articulating exactly what they think about school, and they frequently tell us in compelling, honest, and interesting ways if we are willing to listen. Some of these may sound familiar.

In school . . .

I don't have enough time to finish what I started. That frustrates me.

I can't get it all done. There is too much information in our books.

I can't ask too many questions. We don't have time.

I don't understand some things, and the teacher doesn't have time to help me. There are too many other kids in the classroom who need more help than I do.

I want to have a longer recess, but we can't. I love to play ball with my friends—we teach each other lots of game moves, but that is not on any test.

I am not allowed to talk unless the teacher says I can. I like to talk; it helps me learn.

I have to stay in my seat unless the teacher says I can get up or get in a group. I seem to get ideas faster when I am standing.

I like music and art, but we never really get to do that very much. They are not considered subjects except maybe in junior high or high school clubs.

I like to try things out to see if they work, but it takes too much time for the teacher to prepare that kind of a lesson. She doesn't have enough help to do that, so we just don't do it.

I might not get a good grade in math, because I can't remember formulas very well. If I do extra-credit work, maybe I will pass.

The teacher doesn't really like me because she never calls on me to answer. I don't care either, because I don't always know the answer.

Parent: "What did you learn in school today?" Child: "Nothing," and he is really thinking: "I can't really remember what I learned."

I have too much homework, and if I don't do it, I'll be in trouble.

I wish homework made more sense. The teacher just taught this today, and I can't really practice something that I only saw on the board for fifteen minutes.

I think my teacher doesn't like boys, because she is always yelling at them.

The bell rang before I could finish the test. It was a timed test so I failed it. I really did know the answers; it just takes me a while to think about what I want to write.

We have a science project due in three weeks, but I need help because the teacher wants it done exactly the right way. I am not sure I know the right way.

I am worried about missing school, because when I do the teacher says, "You'll just have to get caught up." How do I do that?

I am not good at getting up in front of the class, but I have to give a speech and if I don't my teacher said he would give me one grade lower than what I would get if I did it in front of the class.

Our team table is winning the extra-recess coupon for getting all the answers right in the Jeopardy game. Some teams will never win, because they don't listen in class very well.

Parent: "If you get all As on your report card you'll earn ten dollars." Child: "What do I have to do to get an A?"

My teachers tell me that life doesn't give you second chances so I'd better get it right the first time. She won't let me do this over. I know my big brother got to take his driver's test four times before they finally gave him a license.

If it doesn't get graded, then why am I doing this?

I used to like school.

Do I have to go to school today?

Why is school so boring?

I hate school.

Are we really listening to what they are telling us? Obviously there are activities that we don't particularly like to do in life. Each of us has our own set of detestable chores. Yet knowing that children have come to equate learning with a detestable chore is troublesome and something is amiss. Until all of the student voices are clearly heard, validated as important, and acted upon, our current school model will not improve.

OUT OF THE MOUTHS OF BABES AND OTHER BRIGHT PEOPLE

A young student speaking to a fellow classmate in the recess line at school was heard saying, "I wish we only had school on the days that don't end in the letter y"—to which his puzzled-looking friend thought for a moment, grinned, and then wildly and loudly agreed, saying the following: "Ahh . . . that would be *no*-day, right?" As the adage says . . . "out of the mouths of babes," or, in this case, fourth-graders.

In 2012, a seventeen-year-old young man named Nikhil Goyal wrote a book titled *One Size Does Not Fit All*, in which he provides an important and often overlooked perspective on the institution of school. His treatise is courageous, gut-wrenchingly honest, and wrought with many morsels of truth. His following statement was sobering and accurate: "Rule of thumb: Never trust anything Secretary Arne Duncan says." After Goyal listened to a town hall speech by President Obama in June 2011, he pronounced that "the president didn't seem to realize that every single one of his previous statements are antithetical to the policies his very own Department of Education has pursued, including the expansion of standardized tests."[1]

This particular example from Goyal's book takes aim at those in public service, even those who are well respected. No matter who the politician, they say what they believe will garner public favor. This practice is bipartisan and frequently flies in the face of real, substantive school reform. It also reflects how a mega-institution, such as the federal Department of Education, often takes on a life of its own. A very scary thought.

John Taylor Gatto, a retired American schoolteacher, makes several compelling assertions in his book *Dumbing Us Down*, which describes what school does "to" children.

Here is his list:

> It confuses the students. It presents an incoherent ensemble of information that the child needs to memorize to stay in school. Apart from the tests and trials, that programming is similar to the television, it fills almost all the "free" time of children. One sees and hears something, only to forget it again.

- It teaches them to accept their class affiliation.
- It makes them indifferent.
- It makes them emotionally dependent.
- It makes them intellectually dependent.
- It teaches them a kind of self-confidence that requires constant confirmation by experts (provisional self-esteem).
- It makes it clear to them that they cannot hide, because they are always supervised.[2]

Gatto experienced a defining moment back in June 1991 when he finally decided to quit teaching in Manhattan after thirty years. At that time, he was also recognized as New York State Teacher of the Year. It just so happened that he wrote a short essay titled "I Quit, I Think" explaining why he decided to "throw in the towel." He sent it off and was told it would be published at the editor's discretion so he quickly forgot about it. On July 5, 1991, he said he "swallowed hard and quit." Twenty days later, his essay was published in the journal.

While the entire essay is worth reading, this sample provides an excellent description of why substantive school reform is so difficult and often not realized.

> School is too vital a jobs project, contract giver, and protector of the social order to allow itself to be "re-formed." It has political allies to guard its marches; that's why reforms come and go without altering much. Even reformers can't imagine school being much different. . . . [I]nitiatives rise from ignorance of how people learn or deliberate indifference to it. I can't teach this way any longer. If you hear of a job where I don't have to hurt kids to make a living, let me know. Come fall, I'll be looking for work. [3]

In his book titled *Weapons of Mass Instruction*, Gatto attempts to slay the schooling beast and provides a courageous plan he calls "The Bartleby Project." The intent was derived from a short story written in 1853 by Herman Melville. Without going into the specific details, the Melville story describes a human photocopying machine, named Bartleby, who suddenly begins to exercise free will and declines to obey an order, to which he replies, "I would prefer not to." [4]

Gatto borrowed the concept and passed it on to his readers, encouraging them to opt out of "required" standardized testing by simply saying, "I prefer not to take the test." [5] As one can determine from this effort, Gatto strongly opposes anything that attempts to "standardize" learning. A standardized test is a onetime, unreliable attempt to quantify learning. These costly and unreliable assessments are used to rank teachers, schools, and states. They are a sacred cow to many, but not worth the hefty price we pay monetarily or in the time it takes to administer them.

Jerry Mintz, cited in chapter 8, is the founder of the Alternative Education Resource Organization (AERO). In the article "The Ten

Signs You Need to Find a Different Kind of Education for Your Child,"
Jerry provides a list of signs that may serve as indicators pointing to a
need for finding alternative schooling for children who exhibit them.
He goes on to say that none of these signs by themselves are reason to
panic. But if several of the ten are noticed, one should consider explor-
ing educational alternatives.[6] The following quote from Mintz's article
details three commonly expressed and experienced signs:

> Does your child say he or she hates school? If so, something is prob-
> ably wrong with the school. Children are natural learners, and when
> they're young, you can hardly stop them from learning. If your child
> says they hate school, listen to them.
>
> Has your child lost interest in creative expression through art,
> music, and dance? Within the traditional system, these creative out-
> lets are often considered secondary to "academic" areas, and are not
> as widely encouraged. In some cases, courses in these areas are not
> even offered any more. This neglect often devalues, or extinguishes,
> these natural talents and abilities in children.
>
> Does your child come home talking about anything exciting that
> happened in school that day? If not, maybe nothing in school is
> exciting for your child. Why shouldn't school—and education—be a
> fun, vibrant, and engaging place?[7]

Alfie Kohn, also mentioned earlier in this book, is well known in the
field of education. He has written many compelling essays and books
addressing some of the practices that occur in our schools on a regular
basis. He points out, with laser-like focus, a rationale for doing school
differently. An interesting quote on a recent blog reads, "Please keep in
mind that phrases such as 'effective policies,' 'higher achievement,'
'better results,' or 'improved outcomes' refer only to scores on standardized tests. These tests are not only poor indicators of meaningful intellectual accomplishment but tend to measure the socioeconomic status
of the students or the amount of time they have been trained in test-
taking skills."[8]

In fall 2015, it was estimated that about 50.1 million students will
attend public elementary and secondary schools. Of these, 35.2 million
will be in prekindergarten through eighth grade and 14.9 million will be
in grades 9 through 12. An additional 4.9 million students are expected

to attend private school.[9] These numbers are noteworthy and provide a compelling urgency for a better plan than a back-to-school bus tour.

A few brave visionaries have begun to tackle the "sacred cows" that are considered the bread and butter of schools. People are listening. As Oliver Wendell Holmes stated, "The mind, once stretched by a new idea, never returns to its original dimensions."[10] These ideas will indeed stretch the minds of many.

The current practices listed in the two subsequent chapters can be actively applied by teachers, administrators, and parents. Others may need discussion and consensus among stakeholder groups in order to move forward. Some will require advocacy on the local, state, or federal level. In any event, there is no time to waste.

There is an opportunity to reimagine our schools and repurpose them on behalf of the millions of children in our country whom they have not served well. It is within our reach to break the cycle of abuse and the stronghold that is suffocating the life and joy out of authentic learning. Compulsory, controlled, and contrived schooling will not be singlehandedly dismantled overnight, and it is not just a public school problem. Any school system that purports to "educate" young people will find the next chapters compelling, and one should read them with an open mind.

10

OUT OF THE BOX

"Any intelligent fool can make things bigger and more complex. . . .
It takes a touch of genius—and a lot of courage to move in the
opposite direction." —Albert Einstein

"If there is a way to do it better . . . find it." —Thomas Edison

RIGOR MORTIS

Rigor mortis (Latin: rigor, "stiffness"; mortis, "of death")[1] is one of the
recognizable signs of death; it is due to chemical changes in the muscles
after death, which cause the limbs of the corpse to stiffen. For many,
school years are a slow death. Death to curiosity, creativity, and excite-
ment. Death to imagination, innovation, and interest. Death to passions, dreams, and hopes. Once the death occurs, the stiffness sets in
and manifests itself as boredom, hopelessness, resignation, apathy, and
indifference. It is a sad but common occurrence. This is a rather dark
analogy, but one that could be made as it pertains to death by schooling.

There is another type of rigor, however, that is often referenced in
schooling. *Merriam-Webster*'s definition doesn't exactly conjure up
happy thoughts:

> Rigors: the difficult and unpleasant conditions or experiences that
> are associated with something. The quality or state of being very
> exact, careful, or strict.[2]

Although the notion of death and rigor seems an appropriate course of action for the dilemma of poor academic student performance, the promises of "common core" threw a multitude of parents and advocacy groups reeling with contempt once they discovered their existence and origin. These groups argue that the "common core" standards were never presented or vetted in an open, inclusive, or transparent dialogue at a local school or district level. Contrary to what the package told us, the standards were not properly vetted at all on the local level. In fact, many teachers and entire school districts were not aware that their state had adopted new standards until quite some time later.

However, common core propaganda finally came to the local level in various formats promising just about everything from improved skills like critical thinking and problem solving to helping children succeed in their future. The new standards also promise to help teachers provide much clearer goals than in the past, claiming that we can now provide more individualized support to students. That is a huge leap of faith.

The common core producers told us that they were developed based on education research and proven best practices from schools across the country, and that they were designed to promote critical thinking and help ensure that our students graduate with the skills they need to be ready for the future. They are sure to mention that the Common Core doesn't dictate the curriculum or lesson plans—our teachers and school leaders still make those decisions.

They insist that the standards were developed by a group of teachers, state governors, and education leaders from forty-eight states. We are told that this group first came together in 2009 to establish learning goals based on education research and existing best practices with a proven track record of student success. We are also told that state participation in the development process was voluntary, and so was the decision to adopt the standards in 2010.

Interestingly, adopting the common core standards was among several conditions tied to receiving large portions of federal dollars (Race to the Top) at a time when every state was languishing in a severe budget crisis. States rushed to adopt these new standards in hopes of gaining a large federal allocation to help ease the upside-down educational budgets across the nation.

Many state departments of education literally presented the information in June 2010 and adopted it by July 2010 with very little fanfare.

As mentioned earlier in the chapter, educators on the local level discovered the new standards long after they had already been adopted at the state level. School districts have spent the last several years preparing and transitioning (and millions of dollars implementing) this initiative, hoping that students would benefit by way of readiness and opportunity for colleges and careers.

The overarching title of "College and Career Anchor Standards" implies, and we have been told, that if we anchor students well enough in these specific learning targets they will produce a solid foundation on which to begin higher education or a technical or trade school with successful outcomes. One of the many problems with this kind of propaganda is the reliability of that claim.

The large-scale dissemination of these common core standards came by way of a script that told us they were internationally benchmarked and their development involved teachers and parents. The following is an excerpt from the California Department of Education website:

> Since 2010, 45 states have adopted the same standards for English and math. These standards are called the Common Core State Standards (CCSS). Having the same standards helps all students get a good education, even if they change schools or move to a different state. Teachers, parents, and education experts designed the standards to prepare students for success in college and the workplace.[3]

While this statement sounds inclusive and promising, it is just not true. Common standards don't equate to all students getting a good education. Additionally, in the case of California and apparently several other states, there were no representative working groups of teachers or parents on this vetting committee.

Here is the scenario: This working group was voluntary, and your state chose not to participate but decided, after a rather quick review, to adopt the common core standards written by others on your behalf. You are ever so thankful to this "working" group deciding what your child will learn that you just accept this gracious gift without question. After all, these are the experts and they know best, right?

Most of the "education experts" referred to in this script were heads of advocacy and policy groups. Those who are actually in the field of education who served in this process acted as rubber stampers on the standards documents that were already created. Several of these re-

viewers are outspoken critics of the common core standards and refused to sign off on them. In a *Breitbart* article written by Susan Berry,
Dr. Sandra Stotsky, one of the professors chosen to validate the new
common English language arts standards, shares her belief:

> We are a very naive people, everyone was willing to believe that the
> Common Core standards are "rigorous," "competitive," "internation-
> ally benchmarked," and "research-based." They are not. . . . Many
> people were quick to believe that the standards were "all those
> things" at least in part because of the fact they were privately backed
> by corporations and, primarily, by the Gates Foundation. In many
> ways, whoever is ultimately behind the Common Core used private
> groups to their advantage. Because Common Core is run by private
> corporations and foundations, there can be no Freedom of Informa-
> tion Act (FOIA) filings or "sunshine laws" to find out who got to
> choose the people who actually wrote the standards. It's completely
> non-transparent and rather shady.[4]

Stotsky also warns us with alarming clarity the impact that this process
implies:

> Local school districts should be suing their state Boards of Education
> for not insisting on the ability to review the standards or on an au-
> thentic validation before accepting them. There was no legal basis to
> accept the standards for the states. The rights and responsibilities of
> local districts were reduced if not taken away by the state board of
> ed's vote to adopt Common Core with all its strings. They didn't
> consult with local school boards first and let them know what they
> were up to before they voted to adopt Common Core. It may be the
> case that the grieving party has to be a student, not a school board.
> But the local level should be complaining loudly and someone should
> be asking for the state board of ed to resign or be put out of exis-
> tence.[5]

A Berkeley mathematics professor, Marina Ratner, speaks out
against the common core mathematics standards in another recent article in *Breitbart* written by Susan Berry:

> Ratner writes that she initially experienced the Common Core stan-
> dards last fall through her then-sixth grade grandson in Berkeley.
> Reviewing her grandson's math homework, Ratner found it followed

the Common Core math standards exactly. Assignments on fractions required drawing pictures of "6 divided by 8, of 4 divided by 2/7, of 0.8 x 0.4, and so forth." "For example, create a story context for 2/3 divided by 3/4 and use a visual fraction model to show the quotient . . ." Ratner reads, and then asks, "Who would draw a picture to divide 2/3 by 3/4?" Noting that, with Common Core, students are continually asked to draw models to answer "trivial questions," Ratner asserts, "A student who gives the correct answer right away (as one should) and doesn't draw anything loses points."[6]

Additionally in this article, Susan Berry says that

Breitbart News asked Dr. R. James Milgram, professor of mathematics at Stanford University—who was asked to be a member of the Common Core Validation Committee but then refused to sign off on the standards—about Ratner's observation regarding Common Core's persistent emphasis on visual models, even for simple questions.

"It is believed by most U.S. math education Ed.D.'s that at-risk students learn better using manipulatives and that the focus of U.S. standards should always be these students," Milgram said. "So they choose pedagogy that effectively turns off the average and even more so the above-average students in a desire to focus on the weakest students."

Milgram observes, however, "The research on how at-risk students learn most effectively is absolutely clear on the fact that this is the worst possible method for teaching these students this material.

"Likewise, the research on gifted students shows that those students learn best when they are allowed to accelerate and learn at their own speed," he adds.

"Finally, over the last century, not one paper in the education literature that has met basic criteria for reproducibility has shown that the kind of group learning pushed in Common Core is more effective than direct instruction," Milgram asserts. "In fact, a close reading of most of these papers seems to indicate that these methods are significantly less effective than direct instruction. Given this, the most likely outcomes are an across-the-board-weakening of student outcomes."[7]

While some believe this effort to be a noble undertaking and a collaborative state-led initiative, many believe that it is the most intrusive and expansive federal attempt thus far to take away local control of education in our states. The dangling carrot of Race to the Top (RttT) funds with its firmly held strings attached sealed the deal with regard to federal involvement. The timing, the requirements, and the overall direction of RttT left a very bad taste in the mouths of many. One such notable critic is Diane Ravitch, former assistant secretary of education, who summed it up quite well: "Race to the Top is NCLB on steroids."[8]

Let's envision these new standards and support structures solidly in place ten years from now. What results could we predict? Instincts and experience tell us that at best this is an experiment with little or no evidence of effectiveness. Students will still learn how to take tests that hopefully produce the desired results and all will not be well with schools. Rather, initially dismal scores will eventually lead to an unimpressive leveling off with the same number if not more students dropping out, opting out, and giving up as a way to reflect what the "schooling" experience did for them.

In the end, contrary to what some believe, school disenchantment has nothing to do with common standards, quality of implementation, teacher training, or enough funding. It has everything to do with our current institution of school itself, which mistakenly equates teaching with learning. As a society, we are duped to believe this.

Alternatives such as publicly funded charter schools are offered up as a way out for some, and yet, even in these cases, results are not stellar or sustainable. Many local school districts mistrust the intentions of any charter group that approaches them. However, charter schools will continue to pop up around the country as a viable option for parents. There are many success stories even among the bad publicity.

The idea of issuing vouchers was seen as undermining the very core of public education in many circles even while the federally funded Title I Program Improvement (PI) sanctions force school choice as a way to escape schools that are deemed as failing. As one moves through the PI trap, sanctions offer one-to-one or small-group tutoring, corrective action, and even restructuring, all within strictly defined methods and procedures that are identified as best practices.

The jewel on the crown of a PI school was to have the state take the school over and reopen it under new management. All this was happening as states were scrambling to jump off the sinking No Child Left Behind (NCLB) ship by way of a restrictive and agenda-driven waiver.

What a sorry state of affairs we have brought to schools and, ultimately, our children across this country. Promises, punishments, threats, and neglect are all part of the schooling system we perpetuate on a regular basis. While Congress has tried to repackage NCLB as a much more "student-friendly" piece of legislation, it's just another federally mandated, top-down intrusion into what should be the freedom to learn as one sees fit. Rogue states who are tired of these federal dollars have just said no to the funding and are schooling their students with state funding sources.

Educational platforms and reform efforts that only provide cursory lip service to a deep-seated problem will never yield the kind of change that is so desperately needed. Don't be duped by a vague list of generalities or so-called strategies as the way to tackle the current schooling issues. The federal department of education is very adept at spreading this kind of propaganda through sound bites given to them by the system itself. Be a savvy citizen and look for the meat, not just a bone tossed in your direction.

Many legislators and advocacy groups demand that a federal education bill be designed to serve the neediest, most marginalized students. This is sought in order to address the problems of inequity. What seems to be grossly misunderstood in the discussion is the belief that an education bill will adequately address or eradicate the entrenched behemoth in our country—*racism*.

While certain legislation is critical and needed, any attempt to harness the human endeavor of learning by way of compulsory testing will result in the lowest common denominator. It has happened before; it will happen again no matter what title one names the bill. What is tested is taught.

In spite of all the efforts, there remain many questionable practices played out in schools on a daily basis. Much of what we do makes absolutely no sense and flies in the face of known educational and developmental learning theory. Great teachers know this well and have been trying for years to get someone in the hierarchy to listen.

In the next two chapters, ten widely accepted and never questioned practices are listed for your consideration. They are grouped into two categories: five factory-model structures and five factory-model processes. These structures and processes will sound familiar. They are more than likely how you remember schooling. Examining these practices more deeply reveals a troublesome and alarming scenario, one that needs immediate attention.

To set the record straight, listing ten common practices and offering alternatives to schooling gone wrong will not magically resolve the issue overnight. Nor is this list exhaustive of all that could be done on behalf of real learning. It is, however, a starting place where known areas of ineffectiveness are highlighted with suggested alternative approaches based on sound educational theory. Much of what we have done in schools up to this point in time has been a monumental experiment. What have we got to lose?

11

TEN "UN"COMMANDMENTS (PART 1)

"We must all face the choice between what is right and what is easy."
—J. K. Rowling, *Harry Potter and the Goblet of Fire*

FACTORY-MODEL STRUCTURES

Grade Levels

For the most part, children who turn five are sent to kindergarten; six-year-olds are first-graders; seven-year-olds are second-graders; and so on throughout the K–12 system. If they "adequately" learn the information, they get to move on to the next grade level; if not, they either repeat the entire year, or they move on with interventions. This is acceptable practice, and no one typically questions it—no one except bright and insightful teachers, administrators, and parents who understand that the developmental progression for each child varies.

Setting an arbitrary end date by way of completing a grade level is ludicrous and flies in the face of everything educators learn in undergraduate psychology courses and have come to understand more clearly from brain research.

One plea from teachers cited more than any other is the need for time—more time to delve deeper into the learning, more time with those students who need more assistance, and more time to plan and collaborate with other teachers on how best to design the learning to ensure that students have what they need. Some teachers "loop" with their students so they can follow the natural progression in learning, but that doesn't resolve the problem of the rigid grade-level configurations.

Sir Ken Robinson titled his TED talk "How Schools Kill Creativity," and although his particular focus was the lack of time and place for the arts and avenues to foster creativity in our schools, he also provided a very compelling history of why this is the case. He explains that we continue to use the factory model to educate children by "batches."[1]

In his TED talk, and in his subsequent book, *Out of Our Minds*, he wittingly says that "students move through the system in age groups as if the most important thing the children have in common is their date of manufacture."[2]

This seems like a no-brainer, yet we ignore it and refuse to make any kind of change in the grade-level schemata except to create combo-classes, which address numbers and staffing more than educationally sound practice. So, we continually have interventions that we must provide, which are costly, time consuming, and demoralizing for the student who needs to receive it. Why is this so? Who really benefits from grade levels?

The educational institution itself benefits in that it makes record keeping and tracking easier. Grade levels are easy to monitor and control. Within the confines of a grade level, standards, curriculum, textbooks, and accounting all provide ease of navigation to all those involved with a "one-size-fits-all" approach. Except, teachers will tell you that the greatest challenge they have is meeting the needs of all the students in their classroom, because they are all at different levels in their learning; some need more time and different resources than others. What a novel concept: learning is different for different people.

Solution: Get rid of grade-level configurations. Group children by clusters of ages, interests, and passions. Let them take as long as they need to understand and grapple with concepts. Let them experiment and remove the words "at risk of failure" from all school documents. Public schools can still claim their Average Daily Attendance (ADA) by age and track attendance by groups. It just takes someone at the state level to think out of the box. This is not hard to do, by the way.

Quotes to Consider

"In fourth grade I had a high school reading level, but I didn't want to go to school and I didn't feel I belonged there." —Freddie Prinze[3]

"Education is not a race, with winners and losers. It's not a commodity to be bought and sold." —Grace Llewellyn and Amy Silver[4]

"I am entirely certain that twenty years from now we will look back at education as it is practiced in most schools today and wonder that we could have tolerated anything so primitive." —John W. Gardner[5]

Bell Schedules

Whistles blowing at the factory signaled a change in shift for start and end times, so bells ringing in schools was a softer version of that practice. Remember the intent was to get young people ready to go to work. How else can we herd a school of, say, seven hundred elementary students or perhaps one thousand young people in a secondary setting through our buildings without chaos or incident? So, the bells stay as a permanent fixture. We can't even imagine life in school without them. But they do exist, at least in some places where they have learned that the bell is unnecessary and disruptive.

Ask a teacher how many times they found themselves at an exciting teachable moment when the bell rang. In my opinion, it sends the wrong signal. Some proponents of these arbitrary practices defend them as necessary skills that children and adolescents must learn supporting their purpose as teaching students about life, a life that has time constraints and deadlines and similar demands.

Seriously? We have to teach students for thirteen years how to properly respond to a bell that will help them meet some future, unknown deadline? Let's face it, our current educational system was built on the factory model, and not much has changed over the past one hundred years.

Solution: Unplug the bells, pull the cord, and turn the timer off. Save money on these wasted systems. When you create classrooms around learning, not time, there is no need for bells. If we worried less about covering material and focused more on the individual needs of each student in whatever time that took, we might just see real learning take place. Teacher teams, working and planning together and teaching in their area(s) of expertise and strength, will help. They can also monitor the time without skipping a beat. Some of you are not convinced. Keep reading.

Quotes to Consider

> "I've noticed a fascinating phenomenon in my thirty years of teaching: schools and schooling are increasingly irrelevant to the great enterprises of the planet. No one believes anymore that scientists are trained in science classes or politicians in civics classes or poets in English classes. The truth is that schools don't really teach anything except how to obey orders. This is a great mystery to me because thousands of humane, caring people work in schools as teachers and aides and administrators, but the abstract logic of the institution overwhelms their individual contributions. Although teachers do care and do work very, very hard, the institution is psychopathic—it has no conscience. It rings a bell and the young man in the middle of writing a poem must close his notebook and move to a different cell where he must memorize that humans and monkeys derive from a common ancestor." —John Taylor Gatto[6]

> "In October 2010 Mackie Academy, in Stonehaven, Kincardineshire took the move to turn off their school bell system, following criticism that the school bells agitated pupils. According to the headteacher the corridors became much quieter after the system was introduced. It was hoped that pupils would take more responsibility for ensuring they arrived on time to lessons. A number of other schools in the United Kingdom have made similar decisions and either partially or completely turned off the school bell system." —Stuart Patterson[7]

Length of School Day and School Year

Schools across the United States typically started after Labor Day for many years and ended sometime in late May or early June with holidays and observances scheduled throughout the school year. This was the traditional agricultural calendar that enabled the children to help with planting and harvesting crops many, many years ago. Since fewer of our current students actually work on a family farm, this outdated model needs to go. Some schools and districts have modified their calendars to be year-round with more frequent times off or on track. Others have modified versions of this tradition.

Funding sources for the schools are tied to ADA, and compulsory school laws tell us that we must attend school for a minimum number of hours a day and days per year. How can we mess with this long-held practice and strongly entrenched belief that the longer we are in school the more we will learn?

Gross productivity and return on investment of time just don't yield positive results that make a substantial difference in student learning. The goal is to allow for the greatest opportunity for learning that is delivered more through equitable access and how we structure the day rather than the number of minutes in the seat.

A whole new approach would include scheduling school hours for shorter periods of time. The school day (four or five hours at most) can be designed for academic pursuits facilitated by the teacher with student input. These pursuits would include frequently scheduled field trips for the younger student and apprenticeship-like schedules for older students. Teachers can rotate monitoring these endeavors and could follow up with students for next steps in their learning plans.

School hours designed around the optimal or peak performance times are different for every child and young person. Some argue that we need to wake children early in order to prepare them for an eight-hour working day. Although many schools require students to attend six or seven hours with breaks for lunch and recess in the lower grades, these longer hours are not necessary.

There is no reliable evidence or research that proves a longer school day yields better learning results. Our circadian rhythms send a very different signal to our brains that a rest period is needed. We also know that young people need a longer sleep period than adults, and teens need even more.

Many of us have heard of the Finland model of education, where students don't start school until they are seven, they rarely take exams or do homework until well into their teen years, and they are not measured at all in the first six years of their education. There is only one mandatory test taken at the age of sixteen. Elementary Finnish students get seventy-five minutes of recess a day compared to the average U.S. student at twenty-seven minutes a day, and teachers spend only four hours a day in the classroom and two hours a week for professional development. Finland consistently outperforms other countries on international assessments of student progress.[8]

Are their children hardwired differently than our children in the United States, or have they discovered optimal learning conditions? Obviously, you can decide for yourself. The evidence for less time in school is very compelling.

More time in school does not necessarily translate into more learning. It can, however, result in burnout or inattentiveness. Rethinking the way we use the allotted time is a much better idea. Internships, project-based learning, and more authentic endeavors are promising alternatives. Students working together to research, design, and create is a lifelong skill they can carry into their chosen field in adulthood.

There is a belief that the school day needs to closely mirror a workday. Many parents may work eight hours with travel time on either end, equaling perhaps ten hours. Typically a student's day averages about seven hours. This leaves some working parents with chil-care needs. If we shorten the day, aren't we creating undue hardship on working parents?

One might consider asking a different kind of question. Does school exist to provide a place for children to be while their parents are at work, or is it built around the optimal learning time for children?

Solution: Minimize the school day to four or five hours. Include frequent activity breaks and more freedom of choice for student interests. The extra time not in contact with students affords teachers a chance to collaborate on student projects, prepare and plan for more authentic and hands-on lessons, and design more individualized support.

Parents in need of child care may access after-school programs either at their child's school, or near it. Many already avail themselves to this option.

Nonmandated schooling hours allows parents the freedom to choose other appropriate options for their children without the threat of punishment by law. The right to learn as one sees fit is a basic principle of liberty that has been taken away and replaced with a one-size-fits-all counterfeit—mandatory schooling and school hours.

Quotes to Consider

"We ask children to do for most of a day what few adults are able to do for even an hour. How many of us, attending, say, a lecture that doesn't interest us, can keep our minds from wandering? Hardly any." —John Holt[9]

"The bits I most remember about my school days are those that took place outside the classroom, as we were taken on countless theatre visits and trips to places of interest." —Alan Bennett[10]

"It is, in fact, nothing short of a miracle that the modern methods of instruction have not yet entirely strangled the holy curiosity of inquiry; for this delicate little plant, aside from stimulation, stands mainly in need of freedom; without this it goes to wrack and ruin without fail. It is a very grave mistake to think that the enjoyment of seeing and searching can be promoted by means of coercion and a sense of duty." —Albert Einstein[11]

Class Sizes

By design, factories produce massive quantities of products or goods for profit. Similarly, industrial-age schools are designed to pack as many students as physically possible into a given space and mass produce an education founded on the principle of compulsory schooling for all. When you place twenty-five to thirty-five and, in some cases, fifty students into a rather small and restrictive environment, common sense tells you there will be problems. Why in the world are we still doing this?

The number one reason for stuffing children into classrooms has nothing to do with education. It is what the educational community calls ADA, or Average Daily Attendance. Schools receive per-pupil dollars to run their programs, pay their employees, build schools, buy buses, and meet their ever-increasing mandated costs. The bigger your system the more money you need, which in some cases equates to hiring fewer teachers and raising class sizes.

No teacher reading this can deny that fewer students in a classroom means greater attention for all, more time to work with small groups or individuals, and more opportunity to meet the unique needs of each child. Every parent knows that this is true as well. The more children in the classroom the less likely your child will be noticed and receive the attention or help he or she needs.

Yet, with alarming regularity we continue to perpetuate and even support the claim that this does not harm children. We believe that good classroom management will cure just about any situation—even lack of space, lack of attention, and lack of common sense. Budgets dictate the number of students in the classroom, not sound educational practice.

What, then, is the magic number for a class size, and how are we ever going to tame the monstrous beast that feeds off of ADA to survive?

Solution: Create classes with no more than fifteen students. Realizing that the whole point of public schooling is economies of scale, the more students we can cram into a classroom the more money we have to pay everyone who works in the school system. However, some practices must supersede others, and class size is one of them. But this is not the only needed change.

Utilize a co-op approach to learning, where groups of teachers share the work and lesson planning based on their area of expertise. Allow students to work in groups or alone as needed. Ensure that the groups are fluid and change frequently. Introducing new concepts to smaller groups with ample time for practice has the potential to create peer experts that can show others who may need a longer period of time to grasp the material. This has been the case in Montessori schools and is quite effective.

And how can we afford that kind of student-to-teacher ratio? From their inception as a factory model, public school systems have created this frustrating dilemma fully aware that classrooms would be bulging at the seams. Apparently, we still have that old factory mind-set, which tells us that herding masses is the goal, not educating them. This is a sad commentary, and one of the most harmful practices.

Quotes to Consider

"When defenders of small classes are asked to produce data to support their case, the first place they turn is a randomized class-reduction experiment conducted in Tennessee in the mid-1980s dubbed Project STAR. Researchers randomly assigned students and teachers in 80 schools to small classes with an average of 15 students or regular classes with an average of 23 students. The students stayed in their randomly assigned category from kindergarten until third grade, when the students in the small classes returned to regular classes. The students in smaller classes tested better—these differences were particularly pronounced among disadvantaged students—and subsequent longitudinal analyses found that the gains followed them through their educational careers. For black students, the higher test scores translated into higher rates of college attendance. But findings like these don't necessarily translate into good policy. Project STAR is the gold standard in class-size reduction literature because it's the only randomized study on the issue that's been conducted since the early 20th century." —Amelia Thomson-Deveaux[12]

The following quote from Matt Chingos, a senior fellow at the Brookings Institution, is rather disheartening considering the dismal state of affairs regarding class size and economies of scale. I provide it as further evidence that there is a sheer lack of will to adequately address this issue in any substantive manner. Rather than figuring out how we can make it work for the good of our children, we just write it off as too expensive and maybe not really worth it after all.

"Reducing class size is one of the most expensive things you can do in education. Even if it does have a substantial positive effect, it still might not be the best use of limited resources." —Matt Chingos, quoted in Amelia Thomson-Deveaux[13]

School Buildings

The idea of sending our young ones off to the school factory every day used to be a comforting thought. Not anymore. School buildings are increasingly becoming targets for crazed and angry individuals with an axe to grind. Of course, this can happen in any building, as we have seen in recent news with movie theaters and government offices and compounds. It is tragic.

Constructing new schools and maintaining older ones is a costly enterprise. Building beautiful schools clearly designed to maximize natural lighting and optimize space is within the reach of some districts, but obviously not all. Families tend to like new shiny schools and "state-of-the-art" campuses complete with science and computer labs. More important, they must have excellent athletic fields and tracks as well as gymnasiums large enough to seat the entire town. The school campus and its buildings are the center of activity in many cases and provide a location for which many local events can occur.

Landscaping, maintenance, and upkeep are constant in order to appeal to families thinking of moving into the area. No one wants an old, falling-apart building with leaking faucets or roofs. The outward structures are supposed to be indicative of what's happening inside.

Again we face a long-held belief that bigger and newer is better. This belief stems from the notion that kids have to spend six or seven hours a day in these places so we need to make them spacious, attractive, and inviting. Until we consider other options, this thought will permeate our paradigm into the future.

Do we really need to go to a place called "school"? Here is the most out-of-the-box idea so far in this list of uncommandments. What if we totally reimagined how we do school and create a network of community participants to open their doors and allow our students in to experience authentic learning on a regular basis? What about online access to learning? What if we met with students and parents to discuss how their students will access their education during the course of a day or week?

There are limitless and exciting possibilities here. A team of forward-thinking, bright people could come up with viable alternatives to sitting at a desk for six to seven hours straight. Learning facilitators or coaches can start the process by brainstorming with the students. Rarely do we ask them what they need or how they learn best. This thought may cause teachers and those working in the current school systems to shudder. How would this work?

The world is full of what-ifs. How sad that we have created a school environment that is predictable and contrived. Just imagine if this were not the case. What would we see, what would we hear, how would our children learn?

Solution: Authentic learning does not typically happen in a staged environment full of distracting posters, classroom desks and chairs, or the typical configuration of a school classroom. Although some rote learning may occur in that kind of environment, getting kids out of a contrived space and into the "world" in which they live will have a much greater impact on their learning and retention of that learning.

Business partnerships with the school community can greatly enhance the learning opportunities for our children and young adolescents, and we should rigorously seek them. While the typical classroom has some limitations, it can serve as a meeting place or workshop space for projects, activities, and events. However, it should not be the only place where we meet with our students.

Teachers would shift their focus to coaching, not teaching, and would come equipped to support a caseload of students who seek them out for their proven coaching skills and similar interests. School buildings may or may not be needed as coaching can be done practically anywhere at any time.

Those entrenched in the current system may be asking some serious questions at this point. Keep in mind, there are really no obstacles that one can't overcome with a little bit of imagination and determination. However, these seem to be a lost art within the current school-based environment that continues to lean heavily upon rote memorization and testing.

Quotes to Consider

"Home schooled children frequently combine for many purposes—and they interact well. The growth of the home schooling movement means that more and more children are learning together, just not in a traditional classroom." —Ernest Istook[14]

"Well-roundedness comes not from sitting in a classroom but from experiencing the larger world." —Alex Tabarrok[15]

"Public school felt like prison—cinderblock walls, fluorescent lights, metal lockers. It was so sterile and unstimulating." —Sufjan Stevens[16]

12

TEN "UN"COMMANDMENTS (PART 2)

"I am beginning to suspect all elaborate and special systems of education. They seem to me to be built upon the supposition that every child is a kind of idiot who must be taught to think." —Anne Sullivan

FACTORY-MODEL PROCESSES

Assessments

It is not unrealistic to consider assessing students, but to what end and for what exact purpose? Many teachers have been brainwashed to think they can't create sound assessments because they are not psychometricians and, therefore, the assessments may be invalid. The fact is that teachers can create effective and authentic assessments without the assistance or hefty price tag of testing companies or data systems. Store-bought assessments are not perfect, nor do they accurately capture all that a student knows or can demonstrate.

Without the misconception that everything has to be assessed and typically via paper and pencil, teachers become empowered to observe and informally assess along the learning continuum. Massive and frequent high-stakes testing has become ridiculously unnecessary and outrageously expensive.

Some say if we don't purchase assessments or assessment systems we won't have reliable data to analyze. Without reliable data, we can't develop goals, and without goals, we won't know where we need to put our efforts. How will we know who is proficient and who is just squeaking by? We would be totally lost and without direction. Well, not actually.

More high-stakes assessments do not equal better student performance; it only ensures that teachers will restrict their teaching to what gets tested. School factory models will continue to pump out student performance results in order to rank schools, rank teachers, and track failing groups of students in order to meet state and federal mandates. And how does any of this benefit students? By the way, it doesn't.

The federal funds received do not equal the ongoing costs necessary to keep the assessment system alive and well. Please keep in mind that the funding is supposed to support the student in need. This same funding comes with heavy restrictions and guidelines on how it must be spent. Hence, there is always a shortfall that must be realized through a school district's general fund.

The federal Every Student Succeeds Act (ESSA), previously known as No Child Left Behind (NCLB), is a disastrous piece of legislation that claims to promote equity, access, and excellence. In fact, it does the opposite. It ineffectively measures only a narrow portion of rote learning. It frustrates the very students whom it was designed to help. It narrows the scope of learning to what is tested and it robs children of precious time.

While the former NCLB requirements mandated that all students meet Adequate Yearly Progress (AYP), the new ESSA still requires schools to annually test every student in grades 3 through 8 and again in high school. They must do this even if they choose not to accept the federal dollars.

Many, including parents, believe that tests are foundational to learning, and they want to see those test results. They took tests themselves and typically don't question the need for assessments, except when they disagree with a score their child received or how the teacher graded it. Testing is simply accepted as a necessary component in the act of schooling, but what is reasonable, purposeful, and an effective way in which to accomplish the goal of assessing student learning?

Solution: Pay the last bill on the district's costly data-management system and use the money for more productive purposes like smaller class sizes, more field trips, and greater access to authentic learning experiences. Assess learning through observation, performance, demonstration, and practical use of skills that have students showing someone else how it is done. This can be very liberating for both the teacher and the student.

Informal classroom assessment is needed, and it is very likely that students themselves can help in the development process. However, the assessments must make sense and be utilized for learning, not grading. Teachers can then be freed up to spend more time coming alongside as a student coach to guide and support them as needed. Feedback during the learning is far more valuable than any high-stakes test. Good coaches know this and so do their students.

As a parent, one way to exercise your rights and send an important message regarding high-stakes testing is to just opt out. Several states already have laws in place that allow for this. Other states are now considering this option given the groundswell of parent pushback on massive, expensive, and ineffective high-stakes testing.

Quotes to Consider

"Now the problem with standardized tests is that it's based on the mistake that we can simply scale up the education of children like you would scale up making carburetors. And we can't because human beings are very different from motorcars, and they have feelings about what they do and motivations in doing it, or not." —Ken Robinson[1]

"Learning happens in the minds and souls, not in the databases of multiple-choice tests." —Ken Robinson[2]

"Assessment becomes 'formative assessment' when the evidence is actually used to adapt the teaching work to meet the needs. Studies show that innovations which include strengthening the practice of formative assessment produce significant, and often substantial, learning gains. These studies range over ages (from 5-year-olds to university undergraduates), across several school subjects, and over several countries." —Paul Black and Dylan Wiliam[3]

Grading

The issue of assessments leads to another seemingly normal and appropriate practice: grading students to determine if they have indeed learned. This one is the proverbial sacred cow when it comes to questionable practices. Years and years of professional malpractice have now become the accepted norm. Grades are elevated to the status of gods having no inherent flaws or imperfections. They are deemed essential for school survival based on a well-respected philosophy—one that says students will not take school seriously if there are no grades.

The sum of who you are in school is your Grade Point Average (GPA). For the younger students, it's the number of As you earned, or in the newer, more standards-friendly reporting, it may be a number or a plus or some other invented symbol that tells you that you have met the target.

Parents are the first to cry out for this system to remain intact, for a number of reasons. First, and typically the most common, it is what they are used to since they were graded the same way in their schooling experience. Second, and perhaps not as prevalent, parents believe that it really tells them how well their child is doing, except when they get a grade other than an A and question how it happened. What exactly does a grade tell us? That depends.

Some would argue that a report card with good grades indicates that a student is learning. Most are fine with that scenario as long as it is a favorable report. In actuality, a grade can mean many different things depending upon what the components are. It is strictly arbitrary, school by school, teacher by teacher, and class by class. What really goes into a grade? Why are we so determined that grades are an accurate measure of what one knows?

This will take a major shift in thinking just to get folks talking about it, let alone making any substantive changes to the current way we grade. Again most teachers will tell you that they did not take or even know of any course on how to grade in their teacher training or undergraduate work. Many will tell you that they didn't have a clue how to set up a grade book and just borrowed ideas from colleagues or relied on how they were graded to help them.

Averages are easy to compute, and breaking the evidence into categories by event (classwork, homework, quiz, test, etc.) is still the most common way teachers set up their grading system. Some have ventured into the world of standards-based grading, where they list a learning target and then assign a grade or point to that in their grade book. While this is a slight move in the right direction it is very time consuming and not really necessary.

Though slightly fewer in number over recent years, many teachers still employ the use of zeros to teach students a lesson or, as they inaccurately call it, giving them what they earned or deserve. Never mind that the zero totally skews the entire compilation of evidence and does not represent what a student knows when averaged with all the other grades. Instead of addressing why the student could not or chose not to complete the work, and giving them another opportunity, they are awarded a zero to "teach them a lesson," and that lesson goes a long way to help them really learn. This is an assumption worth questioning.

Others are more benevolent and offer the coveted "extra"-credit path, where one can redeem what might have been lost on a test or quiz for the chance to make it right. The extra credit is given at a cost and often very sparingly so it doesn't become expected. The challenge is to match the extra credit with the missing bits of evidence to show that actual learning has taken place. This often gets a bit murky.

Examples of extra credit are wide and varied, ranging from participating in class to bringing in canned goods for a school food drive. It can be earned by doing additional work oftentimes having little or nothing to do with the original learning target that created the need for extra credit in the first place. This is a weirdly strange phenomenon that occurs frequently in many classrooms.

(Tongue in cheek): The ultimate evidence one gathers to ensure that children are genuinely learning is when you hear a student say one of the following: "Do I need to know this for the test?" "Does this count for a grade?" "Will this grade affect my GPA?"

We have done an effective job programming our students to work for rewards by way of grades. Students soon learn that only what is tested or graded counts; the rest is optional. Extrinsic motivation is rewarded and promoted as normal. This is not exactly the kind of message we want to send, is it?

Additionally, memorizing facts and figures and practicing skills as the preferred method of instruction is believed to produce the most correct answers. A student who produces the right answer is a good student. Those who don't are forced to repeat the "practice" until they get the right answer. In many cases, they are given a limited number of practices to get it right. If they don't, their grade reflects that. This leads to frustration, disengagement, and, among younger children, may cause tears and unnecessary anxiety.

In a recent Facebook post gone viral, Wendy Bradshaw, an adjunct professor at Mercy College, explains her resignation from the K–12 teaching ranks, citing irreconcilable differences. While the entire post is worth reading, here is a snippet to provide the reader a taste of her disillusionment with the current state of schooling:

> Like many other teachers across the nation, I have become more and more disturbed by the misguided reforms taking place which are robbing my students of a developmentally appropriate education. Developmentally appropriate practice is the bedrock upon which early childhood education best practices are based, and has decades of empirical support behind it. However, the new reforms not only disregard this research, they are actively forcing teachers to engage in practices which are not only ineffective but actively harmful to child development and the learning process. . . .
>
> I just cannot justify making students cry anymore. They cry with frustration as they are asked to attempt tasks well out of their zone of proximal development. They cry as their hands shake trying to use an antiquated computer mouse on a ten year old desktop computer which they have little experience with, as the computer lab is always closed for testing. Their shoulders slump with defeat as they are put in front of poorly written tests that they cannot read, but must attempt. Their eyes fill with tears as they hunt for letters they have only recently learned so that they can type in responses with little hands which are too small to span the keyboard. . . .
>
> Some misbehave so that they will be the "bad kid" not the "stupid kid," or because their little bodies just can't sit quietly anymore, or because they don't know the social rules of school and there is no time to teach them. My master's degree work focused on behavior disorders, so I can say with confidence that it is not the children who are disordered. The disorder is in the system which requires them to attempt curriculum and demonstrate behaviors far beyond what is appropriate for their age. . . .
>
> The disorder is in the system which bars teachers from differentiating instruction meaningfully, which threatens disciplinary action

if they decide their students need a five minute break from a difficult concept, or to extend a lesson which is exceptionally engaging. The disorder is in a system which has decided that students and teachers must be regimented to the minute and punished if they deviate. The disorder is in the system which values the scores on wildly inappropriate assessments more than teaching students in a meaningful and research based manner.[4]

As of October 23, 2015, Wendy Bradshaw had received well over 50,000 likes, with no doubt many more to follow. Why does this resonate with so many? Why aren't we doing something about this? These are tough questions demanding honest and urgent responses.

In order to get good grades, a thing called memorization is a must. In the chapter titled "Getting Teaching and Learning Wrong" from his book *The Schools Our Children Deserve*, Alfie Kohn writes,

> Committing things to memory may train you to be a better memorizer, but there is absolutely no reason to think that it provides any real cognitive benefits. Stuffing facts into your head doesn't help you think better; indeed, the time spent stuffing is time not spent analyzing or inventing or communicating, making distinctions or drawing connections.[5]

Within this book, Kohn quotes William Glasser's opinion regarding memorization: "The world says look it up, don't rely on your memory." Glasser adds, "I would hate to drive over a bridge, work in a building, or fly in an airplane designed by engineers who depended only upon memory."[6]

Kohn adds to the discussion by sharing the following:

> In most situations, information doesn't have to be locked in cranial storage—and most information simply can't be, just because there is so much of it. Memorization is a strategy for taking in material that has no personal meaning. . . . The very fact that you have to memorize it suggests there is something artificial about the whole business.[7]

He continues his chapter listing various and reliable sources that refute the process of memorization. Memorizing is not completely off the table, especially in some of the earlier years; however, just knowing how and when to use this method makes it much more effective. A plethora of worksheets to practice skills is not one of them.

Eleanor Duckworth, a recently retired professor from Harvard University, is quoted as saying: "[K]nowing the right answer requires no decisions, carries no risks, and makes no demands, it is automatic and thoughtless."[8] This is the essence of filling out worksheets. Yet we ask our students to do this almost every day, and then to make matters worse we put a grade on it.

Some say that not grading is too radical a change and parents will cry out for explanation and demand that they get letter grades and percentages and some kind of assurance that their child is learning. Many parents have come to think that how well their child does on their report card has a direct correlation to their status as a parent. You've all seen the bumper stickers that say, "I Am a Proud Parent of an Honor Roll Student." Rarely do we see bumper stickers touting the slogan, "I Am a Proud Parent of an Average Student." Are we less proud when they don't come home with As?

Consider this: If we never had grades and were never told that grades were important, would we still learn anything, and how would we know? But wait! Don't we need GPAs for college entrance? Several universities are moving away from this practice; more need to, and we need to push that envelope as hard as we can.

Solution: Stop giving grades and provide verbal or written feedback instead and allow students to show/demonstrate/apply what they know in new situations. Yes, it takes more time, but if you spend less time grading every single piece of work and filling in grades in a tracking system, you'll have more time to provide verbal or written feedback. Allow students more opportunities to self-evaluate. Stop the practice of telling students what "counts" for a grade. Provide opportunities for students to build their own portfolio of work showing progress.

Quotes to Consider

> "I have decided that learning about anything is awesome, but as soon as you put a grade on it . . . not so much." —Jonathan Nuckols[9]

> "We are all in the business of sales. Teachers sell students on learning, parents sell their children on making good grades and

behaving, and traditional salesmen sell their products." —Dave Ramsey[10]

"We can pay teachers a hundred thousand dollars a year, and we'll do nothing to improve our schools as long as we keep the A, B, C, D, F grading system." —William Glasser[11]

"The freedom to make mistakes provides the best environment for creativity. Education isn't how much you have committed to memory, or even how much you know. It's being able to differentiate between what you know and what you don't." —Anatole France[12]

Restrictive and Limited Academic Curriculum

Sir Ken Robinson asks the question, "What is public education for?" He offers that the purpose has been to produce university professors, but according to him they are not the "high-water mark of all achievement." He jokingly reminds us that "university professors live in their heads and slightly to one side and that academic ability has come to dominate our view of intelligence because universities designed the system in their image." He goes on to tell us an important but overlooked reality of the K–12 school system:

The whole K–12 educational system is a protracted process of university entrance. . . . Many highly talented, creative and brilliant people think they aren't. The thing they may have been good at was not valued, or worse, stigmatized. We need to radically rethink our views of intelligence. . . . [T]he fundamental principles of why we educate our students must be founded on the gift of human imagination.[13]

We need to educate the whole child. Not doing so places our children at a frightening disadvantage, especially when the changing world will require it more and more. Obviously there is a common agreement that children should learn how to read, write, compute, and solve problems. However, teaching isolated subjects without demonstrating their connectedness is a travesty.

Some teachers in the lower grades attempt to make connections among the subjects they teach during the course of a school day, and others do not. It takes more time to plan for that kind of teaching, and it is made more difficult by the textbook industry. When students see and understand the interrelatedness of subjects presented in authentic formats, the likelihood of success as well as retention is greatly increased.

In the upper grades, single-subject teaching credentials restrict and often prohibit integration with other content areas. Great teachers develop thematic lessons with colleagues who understand how valuable this kind of teaching can be for the student. They demonstrate, by their willingness to plan thematically, a strong commitment to doing whatever it takes to help.

Imagination is not valued in our current curriculum. However, getting the right answer is. Rarely do we tell our students to use their imagination. Instead, we tell them to copy, paste, and imitate what we do. You can see this in a classroom where all the displayed student work is identical or very similar. The curriculum leaves little to no room for a budding imagination. Is it any wonder why kids are frequently turned off to what we are asking them to do? We also tend to ignore the fact that there are multiple kinds of intelligences and many different ways one is smart.

A cry heard a few years back, and to some extent today, is a return to the basics. What the basics actually means may vary among individuals and groups. Basic and narrow curriculum that focuses solely on reading and math to the exclusion of everything else is restrictive and limiting.

To a great extent, schools are providing the minimum, and yet demanding the maximum, by way of test scores and young people ready for college and careers. Canned reform efforts that percolate up to the mainstream every few years claim to be the agents for change in our schools. One is left wondering, with little to no substantial evidence to prove these claims are true. We are a country of bright and innovative people. Surely we can see through this facade.

Unfortunately, we are in a time in public schooling where common standards have prescribed a set formula for what and how we must teach and what and how students must learn. The problem with most standards is their sheer volume and complexity. Since they did not develop the standards themselves, most teachers look for someone to help them interpret and provide examples of what the new standards are asking of the students.

States produced the standards documents and passed them on to the schools. It is not uncommon for schools or entire districts to seek out

professors or consultants to explain the new standards in a more stu-
dent- and teacher-friendly way. By the way, these professors and consultants didn't write the standards, either. The best they can do is offer
their perspective and understanding. When you have a question, there
is no one to call who actually wrote the new common core standards.
There is no "Common Core Hotline." So how common are they, when
teachers are left to varying degrees of interpretation?

Although the writers of these standards insist that they do not tell
teachers how to teach, they most certainly do. The proponents of the
new standards say that they promote the kind of thinking that has been
lacking in our current models of teaching and learning. However, as
stated earlier, they do not address the overarching problem of the way
in which we *do* school. The standards simply drive what the curriculum
will be.

Solution: If you are a parent, become actively involved in the local,
state, and federal educational arena. Read and learn about educational
alternatives and be courageous. You have nothing to lose and everything
to gain for your children and their future. Examine the curriculum in
your child's school, ask questions, and speak to your local school board;
you are afforded that right.

If you are a school board member, advocate for the whole curriculum, including the arts, and commit funds to support them. Authorize
the staff to innovate and promote out-of-the-box options to achieve
more authentic learning. Allow for greater flexibility on how this is
achieved. Don't rely on high-stakes testing as an indicator of learning. It
is flawed and skewed to rank students based on socioeconomic status,
and it is not a reliable indication of true learning.

If you are a teacher, be involved in the work of curriculum writing at
your school or district. Examine the way textbooks are written and
branch out to include many other sources of learning for your students.
If you solely rely on a textbook to guide your curriculum, you are guar-
anteeing the lowest common denominator for your students. Ask yourself, "Would this be acceptable for my own child?" Then do the right
thing. Share and plan the workload with your teaching team.

Quotes to Consider

> "Most learning is not the result of instruction. It is rather the result
> of unhampered participation in a meaningful setting. Most people

learn best by being 'with it,' yet school makes them identify their personal, cognitive growth with elaborate planning and manipulation." —Ivan Illich[14]

"I can only speak for myself, but public school did nothing for me musically. I got the impression a musical career was frowned upon. But in the arts, resistance can often be the strongest inspiration." —Charlie Fink[15]

"I suggest that the introductory courses in science, at all levels from grade school through college, be radically revised. Leave the fundamentals, the so-called basics, aside for a while, and concentrate the attention of all students on the things that are not known." —Lewis Thomas[16]

Teacher-Centered Instruction

Learning is a social act and involves mostly all of the five senses, yet we rarely allow for that in the classroom setting. Teachers who design their learning environment around the student and how they process the world around them ensure a greater likelihood that students will indeed learn.

Unfortunately, most classroom environments are either too sterile or too stimulating. They are too sterile in the configuration and rigidity. They are too stimulating with every single wall space covered with posters and pictures. Walls are filled with carbon copy, colorful art projects and paragraphs written by students on the exact same topic. Good teachers were taught to do this, by the way. It is supposed to make the students proud of their accomplishments. These practices are not necessarily bad; they are just not necessary for learning.

Teachers are told to make the classroom look inviting. Making it look exciting and actually being an exciting learning place can be two very different realities. The problem is that a classroom is not an ideal place in which to learn because it is devoid of anything authentic. Although we hope it would be a place where learning comes alive, it is really nothing more than a box that holds chairs, desks, supplies, and materials. It is very limiting, confining, and a breeding ground for germs.

Student-centered, authentic learning is the key to unlocking the real potential in every child. More field trips built into the school day and fewer days sitting in a classroom can actually enhance learning. Although field trips tend to have associated costs, these costs are greatly minimized through the use of school funds, foundations, and business and community donations.

Contrary to what we are led to believe, most children and young people don't need a total reliance on the teacher to direct their learning. While the teacher may provide guidance, support, and feedback, most students can discover and learn without prompting. In the first few years of schooling, direct support from a teacher can be beneficial and necessary.

With older children, the structure of teacher as facilitator/coach, guiding and supporting students in their learning, is optimal. This allows the students to own their learning and to actively participate in assessing themselves.

Student-centered instruction requires a shift in thinking as well as a shift in hierarchy from the teacher being the most important person in the classroom to the student being the most important. No matter how hard they try, teachers simply cannot impart knowledge from their brains to their students' heads by standing and delivering. Young people learn best in an authentic setting where they find relevance and meaning for themselves.

Solution: Start the school year with one teacher for the younger children; then as the children grow older and more independent, use a team of teachers based on the teachers' experience and expertise. Consider student-initiated topics of interest and build the curriculum around those interests. Provide as much individual choice as possible, and vary the methods in which students can decide how they want to learn and show what they learned.

Offer support and guidance with needed information and scaffolding. Allow the students to create their learning space environment in the classroom. Work with masters in the field to visit your classroom, or better yet, take the learning outside of the classroom as often as possible.

Quotes to Consider

> "The answer is not to standardize education, but to personalize and customize it to the needs of each child and community. There is no alternative. There never was." —Ken Robinson[17]

"Everybody around the world wants to send their kids to our universities. But nobody wants to send their kids here to public school." —Walter Annenberg [18]

"I never teach my pupils. I only attempt to provide the conditions in which they can learn." —Albert Einstein [19]

Teacher Tenure and Unions

How is it that in every walk of life and in every profession you remain employed only if you are doing your job but in schools this is not the case? When practices are called into question and improvement is warranted, there are monumental "hoops" to jump through that often lead to little change.

In the movie *Waiting for Superman*, this phenomenon was described as the "dance of the lemons,"[20] where ineffective teachers are just danced out of one school into another without any real consequence. In reality, this does happen, and it is a travesty.

Imagine your doctor, dentist, or other health service provider maintaining their professional status while making frequent errors, miscalculations, inappropriate diagnoses, or refusing to serve patients during scheduled office hours. How long would they remain as your provider of choice? Under these circumstances, what would you do? Would you recommend them to your friends and family, or would you shop for a new provider, one who meets your needs and understands your specific condition?

It is important to note that there are many hardworking, ethical, and passionate teachers who would never think of damaging their students. No sincere teacher does. However, when situations arise from time to time where that passion is lost, or was never there to begin with and ethical behavior shifts to unethical, something must be done.

More school districts around the country are calling on teachers via their unions to sit and talk about how we can improve schools together. Often the two sides see it differently. Teachers want increased pay, fewer students in a classroom, and greater autonomy. Management wants improved performance from both the teacher and their students with an accountability plan in place to ensure that happens.

The cycle repeats itself every year during negotiation time. It will continue in this manner as long as there is management and rank and file. This is the hallmark of the industrial-age public school model that has persistently lingered and helped to produce mediocracy, apathy, and indifference.

Teachers are often heard saying that they want to be treated as professionals. Typically they want the freedom to do what they believe is best for each child in their care. They want an equal voice at the table that is respected and valued. Teachers are the practitioners who understand the day-to-day challenges and triumphs in their schools. They know firsthand what is working and what is not. Their voice is critically important to the overall quality of any school or district.

The greatest interest each of us who work in schools can own is the will and determination to provide the best learning conditions for every child who enters the schoolhouse doors. Unfortunately, the truth is that schools don't offer *the best*; they offer what they think they can comfortably afford. But rather than offer no hope on this issue, let's examine what we might do.

Solution: Consistently work to build common goals and always remain transparent. On a regular basis, create common interest lists to work from that always address "children" first. Although teachers may often have a different view from management on how best to address children first, highlighting the common areas and working toward that end is a great start. It is important to build trust, respect, and fairness within the system that are visibly modeled and supported by everyone involved.

Schools created by like-minded individuals with autonomy to focus on authentic and meaningful student learning rarely need negotiations to accomplish their goals. When schools are built on strong student-centered practices, they will accomplish far more than a negotiation session ever will. However, when unions are recognized and function as student-centered advocates, they contribute greatly to improving the overall system itself.

Quotes to Consider

"My mom was a teacher—I have the greatest respect for the profession—we need great teachers—not poor or mediocre ones."
—Condoleezza Rice[21]

"I had teachers who I could tell didn't want to be there. And I just couldn't get inspired by someone who didn't want to be there." —Hilary Swank[22]

"My problem with unions is they breed mediocrity." —Kevin O'Leary[23]

13

THE RECOVERY PROCESS

"We cannot solve problems by using the same kind of thinking that created them." —Albert Einstein

OLD SCHOOL

The previous two chapters outlined just a few of the many practices that could be improved on behalf of our school-aged children. After reading the ten uncommandments, one might ask, what is left? This is a systematic dismantling of the very fabric and structure of most schools as we know them. That is exactly the point. This is not your typical how-to-fix-our-failing-schools treatise that offers first-aid or myopic approaches to a severely bleeding patient. This is a necessary and critical departure from what most have offered and few would condone as feasible.

Where do we start, and how can we make substantive changes that people will understand and support? We know that those who hold the purse strings to the public funds for schools won't take kindly to our efforts to do away with what they have helped to build. We know that some will take the homeschool route, which is a good option. Others will pay large tuition checks for their children to attend a private or church-affiliated school, and that is their choice. What about all those who depend on the publicly funded model of schooling? Why not create the best educational experience we can with what we already know is possible?

This kind of change is grassroots, not orchestrated from the top down. Therefore, we need to involve teachers, parents, and local and state school boards. We need to rally like-minded individuals and families and begin the process of reimagining our schools from the inside out.

It is hard to imagine this well-established institution of public education making any significant structural or impactful changes in the very near future and maybe not in our lifetime. The state and federal networks are so strongly wired to function in a certain way that any attempt to disturb, dismantle, or deregulate would send the whole "school" universe into a tailspin. It is simply too gigantic, too ingrained, too dependent, and too inflexible. This kind of change is not totally out of reach, but it takes persistence and out-of-the-box thinking to unravel the tight knots that time, stubbornness, and denial have created.

What is the answer, then, to this compelling evidence that points to the need for change? Several have addressed this question with soul-searching diligence and have spent their lives devoted to researching and discovering the many possibilities children have for how they choose to learn: ways that make sense to them; that provide meaning, authenticity, and sustainability; and ways that align well with how the human mind learns best. We can learn from their efforts.

Much of the negative discourse around schooling stems from the lack of choice. Public schooling can't be the only player in the game, and it can't be a fallback for those who can't afford better. There must be viable options, and we must embrace them on behalf of all learners.

The Salvation Army had employed a twelve-step process to help addicts overcome their addictions by affirming a pledge as part of their steps to recovery. As with other unhealthy addictions, typically the first step is to recognize that there is a problem. If you are not aware by now, be assured there are many problems with our public schools. They are rampant and widespread and they permeate every level of the institution, so much so that it would take intense efforts of seismic proportions to shake loose the clutching grips of this fundamentally flawed system.

Just as addictions grip their victims and render them helpless, so does the addiction of our current institution of schooling in the United States. We need to shake loose the grips that hold our students hostage to a minimal learning experience at best and move on to recovery with all diligence and speed before we suffer more casualties. What can we do?

First and foremost, in the spirit of recovery, we must admit that our current model of schooling is ineffective, restrictive, and grossly inadequate to ensure and measure authentic and meaningful learning for all students. Second, we must commit to being part of an increasingly important movement of parents, educators, and community members who value freedom and choice, and who are willing to speak and act on that commitment.

In addition, we must be a positive force and influence to bring about a sensible and vitally important change to the system. This can be done in many ways on different levels. An obvious and impactful force is active involvement in local government from the school board level to cities, counties, and states as elected servants with a strong and empowering student-centered platform. Many opportunities exist for needed and important involvement that can make a positive impact and difference.

Our greatest challenge lies in our ability to provide viable alternatives and solutions, not just complaints and arguments. While many schooling critics have done an excellent job pointing out the flaws in the system, few have offered valid solutions or a clear path on how to get there.

As a parent or grandparent, you must become involved, taking full responsibility for the education of your children to the best of your ability. Whether you decide on homeschooling, un-schooling, or private or public schooling, know that you can make a huge difference by your active involvement. Identifying your area of passion and, more important, your child's, can set the stage for real and lasting change. Here are a few ways in which you might consider becoming involved:

Take Action

- Become better informed by asking questions about the practices at your child's school examined in this book.
- Ask for access to school board policies and attend meetings. Be a positive and respectful voice in garnering allies.

- Promote and support the use of local and state resources/revenues to create a menu of educational options for our children and young people.
- Support and encourage educational choices—one size does not fit all.
- Seek, promote, and support local business partnerships with public, private, and homeschool families through mentoring, teaching, and apprenticeship programs.
- Support and endorse candidates who promote school choice and the use of local and state funding to create educational networks for parents.
- Support or volunteer to provide interest-based learning options for young people out of the school setting.
- Write, e-mail, contact, and visit colleges and universities to advocate for strengthening and diversifying teacher preparation courses and entrance requirement options.
- Examine, explore, and utilize online courses in lieu of seat time in school and advocate for their acceptance as credit for course work.
- Visit and volunteer in your local public schools; run for school site councils, PTA, and local school boards to effect positive and lasting change.
- Consider starting a grassroots effort in your community to present these ideas at public meetings or to enlist the support of an advocacy group to speak on your behalf.
- Support local and national advocacy groups that strive to improve the educational options for students.
- Support candidates who believe in and work toward dissolving the federal Department of Education's overreaching mandates.
- Support and advance the cause of ending the practice of compulsory education by allowing parents the right to determine the educational path for their children without sanctions or restrictions.
- Support efforts to eliminate or drastically reduce massive wholesale high-stakes testing and opt out of them as desired.
- If you are a schoolteacher or administrator, become informed, make sound and child-centered decisions, and changes that improve learning for students in your classroom, school, and district.
- Support school choice in the spirit of freedom and partnerships whether public, private, homeschooling, or un-schooling.

WHAT CHOICES DO WE HAVE?

Many families are trapped in a system that seems inescapable. Some single-parent families challenged with time, logistics, and few options have come to rely on public schools to educate their young ones. Some families living in poverty or children of the foster system who are not certain of their future beyond today are dependent upon their public schools to provide a good education. Homeless children and families struggling every day just to survive count on schools to teach and guide their children toward a world of better opportunities.

These and many other families and children depend on the public schools to provide much-needed security, basic meals, support, nurturing, and educational direction in the midst of an adversity beyond what most of us encounter on a day-to-day basis. Some have argued that the ideas proposed in this book would work well for those of means who have control over their situation and can afford to consider other options. But what about those who don't have these same options? What choices do they have?

All children deserve better than what we are currently providing for them. All children deserve to have conditions in which they can thrive, grow, and learn without fear of threat, intimidation, failure, or coercion. All children deserve to learn in a safe environment that nurtures their individualism and supports their interests while enabling them to become independent, creative, and productive young people.

This is no less true for children affected by poverty, racism, or zip code. In fact, it is critically important to ensure that these conditions readily exist for children impacted by these overwhelming obstacles.

Children are not simply to be contained—they need to be freed in order to discover their gifts and passions and the world around them. Public schools can do this. A first step is to *build strong relationships* with children and their families, not as their saviors, but as allies in the quest for authentic, relevant, and enduring learning.

Second, *create conditions in and out of the classroom that promote a learn-by-doing approach*, where students actively engage in discovery, curiosity, and creativity raising the current bar of expectations. Connect them to the world around them instead of isolating them in a school building.

Finally, emphasize and *promote creativity, imagination, and innovation that requires children to think, problem solve, and persevere* rather than waiting as passive receptacles for the teacher to impart all knowledge. All schools can experience this kind of learning if we make up our minds that we will really do whatever it takes to make it happen.

WHAT DO WE REALLY MEAN BY "WHATEVER IT TAKES"?

The catchphrase "whatever it takes" became immensely popular several years ago as the educational slogan du jour. It was launched by keynote conference speakers and writers as schools learned a new and exciting idea called Professional Learning Communities (PLCs).[1] Not a new idea, by the way, just a resurge of energy around an old concept. The concept and catchphrase took off and lodged itself firmly in most schools in the country, much to the amazement and delight of the authors who first coined the phrase.

By its design, a PLC is supposed to ask four important questions as they go about doing the work of educating our children. The questions are "What do you want students to learn and be able to do, how will we know they've learned it, what do we do when they haven't learned it, and what do we do when they already know it?" If we sincerely asked these questions every day, built our delivery systems based on these questions, and functioned within the realm of possibilities this kind of questioning provides, the results would be truly astounding.

PLC work is important and one step closer to teacher autonomy in the planning and implementing of a meaningful school curriculum. It is a joy to watch teachers eagerly plan and work with each other to bring about quality learning experiences for their students. Given the confines of the system, the quick forty-seven-minute period, the malfunctioning technology, the crammed classrooms, and the lack of site funds to take more field trips, teachers researching incredibly inventive ways to share information and get their students engaged and responsible for their own learning is nothing short of amazing.

Teachers coaching their students with a degree of freedom and a genuine invitation to think out of the box is incredibly empowering for both the teacher and the student. There will always be great and dedicated teachers, the ones who hardly notice the time passing because, as Sir Ken Robinson would say, they are "in their element."[2] Their passion for learning far outweighs the rigid system that works against them and their students. They simply love what they do and they do whatever it takes.

In the quest for higher and more effective educational accountability, the ideas presented in this book open a much-needed dialogue with a sharp and relentless focus. It has been far too long that we as a nation have ignored our failing school model with such disregard and apathy. It is mind-numbing and incredulous that reform efforts, legislated mandates, or additional funding will solve the current schooling crisis in our nation.

We, the people, need to take full ownership of this enterprise called school. We must earnestly and tactically strive to resolve the damage that has been done. Hopefully, this book is a wake-up call for all of us, including teachers, to listen to the voices of our children, and to follow those voices as a directional compass that will lead us to a better place.

The freedom to choose ensures the freedom to learn. As Dr. Seuss tells us in *The Lorax*, "Unless someone like you cares a whole awful lot, nothing is going to get better, it's not."[3]

CONCLUSION

Finding Our Moral Compass

"Tell me and I will forget, teach me and I may remember, involve me and I will learn." —Benjamin Franklin

CHOICES

Some public education employees fear that they will cease to exist if too many options are available, but we know now that the one-size-fits-all approach has not worked well for quite some time. Choice is always good. Choice brings freedom. Choice liberates and educates. This is not a political issue but a moral one steeped in the notion that access to learning is a fundamental human right. Controlling the learning of another is not freedom and not a basic principle of liberty. We must have choice; however, we must choose wisely.

Choice is where the problem squarely lies. Many loving families provide a solid and secure beginning where children learn and thrive and excel. They also have the power to make choices. That, however, is not true across the board. Whatever the reason, whether poverty, apathy, or ignorance, we are facing one of the greatest and most heartbreaking educational challenges of our time. Choice is the missing piece and the one important factor that keeps many young children oppressed. It is for these children that we must find a way to make our public schools work better.

The old paradigm of a fairly small classroom filled with too many children/adolescents and too little freedom of choice is a factory model that has not yielded the kind of learning that lasts beyond the tests. The sad commentary is that many believe this is okay. Many of us know all too well that it is just not good enough, and it will never be good enough if kids continue to drop out or become marginalized or, worse, end up totally unprepared for life and career with dreams and hopes unrealized. This happens on a regular basis in schools every day, and we chalk the casualties up to our litany of excuses.

We find ourselves at the intersection of perplexing thought, where the old school paradigm and the new school consciousness collide. We are faced with choices that will either prompt us to keep our current school box or pitch that one in favor of a whole new paradigm. How we proceed from this point on will determine the ease or difficulty with which we continue our journey. The status quo is the easy way, and for many that is what you will choose. That's okay because you read with an open mind, considered what was presented, and decided what you believe is best for you, your child, or your students. At the end of the day, you are the one who holds the cards. Hopefully your choice will make you a winner.

Others may choose to swim upstream, and that will not be easy. But there will be others who will swim along with you . . . others who will cheer you on and support your efforts. Thinking out of the box on matters so fundamentally accepted as normal and hardly questioned is a formidable undertaking, not for the fainthearted. As stated earlier in this book, it requires the three Cs—courage, conviction, and commitment: courage to question the status quo and confront the stark realities that do exist, conviction to rediscover the joy of learning and how important that is, and commitment to be a voice and an active advocate for a much-needed change.

Educational freedom for all students is a must, not an option. Parents and educators want a better system for their children and students. On behalf of the millions of children whose voices have been silenced for too long, it is time to change direction. Our children are depending upon us. We owe it to them.

NOTES

2. THE KINDERGARTEN EXPERIMENT

1. Ann Taylor Allen, "American and German Women in the Kindergarten Movement, 1850–1914," in *German Influences on Education in the United States to 1917*, ed. Henry Geitz, Jürgen Heideking, and Jurgen Herbst (Cambridge: Cambridge University Press, 2006), 85–102, accessed September 27, 2015, www.cambridge.org/us/academic/subjects/history/american-history-general-interest/german-influences-education-united-states-1917.

2. Jessica Barr, "The Philosophy of Education," Froebel Web, 2002, accessed September 15, 2015, www.froebelweb.org/web2005.html.

3. Ellen Berg, "Kindergarten," *Encyclopedia of Children and Childhood in History and Society*, Faqs.org, 2008, accessed September 27, 2015, www.faqs.org/childhood/Ke-Me/Kindergarten.html.

4. Christina Samuels, "Just 15 States Require Students to Attend Kindergarten," *Education Week*, September 19, 2014, accessed August 7, 2015, www.huffingtonpost.com/2014/09/19/kindergarten-laws_n_5851724.html.

5. Ibid.

6. James Hamblin, "Exercise Is ADHD Medication," *Atlantic*, September 29, 2014, accessed October 30, 2015, www.theatlantic.com/health/archive/2014/09/exercise-seems-to-be-beneficial-to-children/380844/?utm_content=buffer5e760&utm_medium=social&utm_source=facebook.com&utm_campaign=buffer.

3. EIGHT YEARS OF *THIS?*

1. Alfie Kohn, "Moving beyond Facts, Skills, and Right Answers," Alfie-Kohn.org, accessed July 21, 2015, www.alfiekohn.org/article/moving-beyond -facts-skills-right-answers/, originally published in "Getting Teaching and Learning Wrong," in *The Schools Our Children Deserve*, by Alfie Kohn (Boston: Houghton Mifflin, 1999).

2. Ken Robinson, "Three Principles That Our Education Systems Are Based," Twitter, June 21, 2015, https://twitter.com/ukedchat/status/612583280500678656.

5. SCHOOL *DAZE*

1. Ken Robinson, *The Element: How Finding Your Passion Changes Everything* (New York: Penguin, 2009), xi.

2. Alfie Kohn, *Punished by Rewards: The Trouble with Gold Stars Incentive Plans, A's, Praise, and Other Bribes* (New York: Houghton Mifflin Harcourt, 1993), 13–14.

6. SCHOOLS OF EDUCATION

1. *Bloom's Taxonomy* is a hierarchical framework for categorizing learning goals. The three overarching categories are identified as: Knowledge, Skills, and Attitudes. Most teacher preparation programs will include the study of this framework as it applies to teaching and learning.

2. *Maslow's Hierarchy of Needs* is a psychological theory that focuses on five stages of growth in human beings. These are described as patterns of emotions that human motivations generally move through. Higher education students majoring in Psychology, Sociology, or Education typically study this hierarchy as it applies to their prospective careers.

3. Randall B. Lindsey, Laraine Roberts, and Franklin Campbell Jones, *The Culturally Proficient School: An Implementation Guide for School Leaders* (Thousand Oaks, CA: Corwin Press, 2005), xviii.

4. Ibid.

7. LEADERSHIP LESSONS

1. Michael Planty, William Hussar, and Thomas Snyder (National Center for Education Statistics) and Grace Kena, Angelina Kewal-Ramani, Jana Kemp, Kevin Bianco, and Rachel Dinkes (American Institutes for Research), "The Condition of Education 2009," National Center for Education Statistics, May 28, 2009, accessed September 29, 2013, https://nces.ed.gov/pubsearch/pubsinfo.asp?pubid=2009081.

2. Kelsey Sheehy, "Homeschooled Students Well-Prepared for College, Study Finds," *Huffington Post*, June 1, 2012, accessed September 2, 2014, www.huffingtonpost.com/2012/06/01/homeschooled-studentswel_n_1562425.html.

3. Ibid.

4. Ibid.

5. Ibid.

6. Planty et al., "The Condition of Education 2009."

7. Ibid.

8. Danielle Douglas-Gabriel, "The Controversial Idea That Could Lower Student Debt," *Washington Post Blog*, December 2, 2014, accessed January 15, 2015, www.washingtonpost.com/blogs/wonkblog/wp/2014/12/02/why-so-many-students-are-spending-six-years-getting-a-college-degree/.

9. Ibid.

8. EXPOSING THE TRUTH

1. United States Department of Education, "Four Ways to Stay Connected to Our 2015 Back to School Bus Tour," *Homeroom* (blog), accessed August 30, 2015, http://blog.ed.gov/2015/09/four-ways-to-stay-connected-with-our-2015-back-to-school-bus-tour/.

2. Maryland State Board of Education, "Maryland Public Schools Suspension by School and Major Offense Category: In-School and Out-of-School Suspensions and Expulsions 2012–2013," Maryland State Board of Education, October 20, 2013, accessed July 19, 2015, www.marylandpublicschools.org/MSDE/divisions/planningresultstest/doc/20122013Student/susp13_sch_comb.pdf.

3. California Department of Education, "Suspension and Expulsion Report," Data Quest, 2014, accessed July 19, 2015, http://dq.cde.ca.gov/dataquest/SuspExp/umirsedcode.aspx?cYear=201314&cType=ALL&cCDS=00000000000000&cName=Statewide&cLevel=State&cChoic=

UMIRS&ReportCode=UMIRS.

4. California Department of Education, "Truancy Report," Data Quest, 2014, accessed July 9, 2015, http://dq.cde.ca.gov/dataquest/SuspExp/TruancyReport.aspx?cYear=201314&cType=ALL&cCDS=00000000000000&cName=Statewide&cLevel=State&cChoic=TruRate&ReportCode=TruRate.

5. Jerry Mintz, "The Ten Signs You Need to Find a Different Education for Your Child," Alternative Education Resource Organization, October 12, 2015, accessed November 15, 2015, www.educationrevolution.org/store/thetensigns/.

6. John Holt, *Instead of Education: Ways to Help People Do Things Better* (Boulder, CO: Sentient Publications, 2004), 207–8.

9. VOICES FROM THE FIELD

1. Nikhil Goyal, *One Size Does Not Fit All: A Student's Assessment of School* (New York: Alternative Education Resource Organization, 2012), 78–79.

2. John Taylor Gatto, *Dumbing Us Down: The Hidden Curriculum of Compulsory Schooling* (Gabriola Island, BC: New Society Publishers, 2005), 2–11.

3. Lisa Nielson, "I Am No Longer Willing to Hurt Children—John Taylor Gatto (A Compilation)," *The Innovative Educator* (blog), January 18, 2011, accessed October 11, 2014, http://theinnovativeeducator.blogspot.com/2011/01/i-am-no-longer-willing-to-hurt-children.html.

4. John Taylor Gatto, *Weapons of Mass Instruction: A School Teacher's Journey through the Dark World of Compulsory Education* (Gabriola Island, BC: New Society Publishers, 2010), 203.

5. Ibid., 205.

6. Jerry Mintz, "The Ten Signs You Need to Find a Different Education for Your Child," Alternative Education Resource Organization, October 12, 2015, accessed November 15, 2015, www.educationrevolution.org/store/thetensigns/.

7. Ibid.

8. Alfie Kohn, "Just Another Brick in the Wall: How Education Researchers Ignore the Ends to Tweak the Means," AlfieKohn.org, June 4, 2014, accessed July 19, 2015, www.alfiekohn.org/blogs/brick/.

9. United States Department of Education, "Institute of Educational Sciences IES," National Center for Education Statistics, March 2015, accessed September 29, 2015, http://nces.ed.gov/fastfacts/display.asp?id=372.

10. Oliver Wendell Holmes, *Goodreads*, 2015, accessed August 6, 2015, www.goodreads.com/quotes/37815-the-mind-once-stretched-by-a-new-idea-never-returns.

10. OUT OF THE BOX

1. *Merriam-Webster Dictionary*, "Rigor Mortis," *Merriam-Webster Dictionary*, 2015, accessed August 19, 2015, www.merriam-webster.com/dictionary/rigor%20mortis.

2. *Merriam-Webster Dictionary*, "Rigor," *Merriam-Webster Dictionary*, 2015, accessed August 19, 2015, www.merriam-webster.com/dictionary/rigor.

3. California Department of Education, "Common Core State Standards," California Department of Education, March 7, 2016, accessed July 10, 2015, www.cde.ca.gov/re/cc/.

4. Susan Berry, "Education Expert Dr. Sandra Stotsky: Common Core 'Rather Shady,'" *Breitbart*, January 16, 2014, accessed September 1, 2014, www.breitbart.com/big-government/2014/01/16/expert-dr-sandra-stotsky-on-common-core-we-are-a-very-naive-people/.

5. Ibid.

6. Susan Berry, "Berkeley Math Professor Ratner: Common Core 'Will Move U.S. Closer to Bottom in International Ranking,'" *Breitbart*, August 6, 2014, accessed September 1, 2014, www.breitbart.com/big-government/2104/08/06/berkeley-math-professor-ratner-common-core-will-move-u-s-closer-to-bottom-in-international-ranking/.

7. Ibid.

8. Diane Ravitch, interview by *School of Thought*, PBS, 2016, accessed September 1, 2014, www.thirteen.org/eye-on-education/diane-ravitch/#.UTt6Cdacdrg.

11. TEN "UN"COMMANDMENTS (PART 1)

1. Ken Robinson, "How Schools Kill Creativity," Computer Users in Education, 2007, Monterey Technology Conference.

2. Ken Robinson, *Out of Our Minds: Learning to Be Creative* (West Sussex: Capstone Publishing, 2011), 57.

3. Freddie Prinze, "Freddie Prinze Quotes," BrainyQuote, 2014, accessed August 8, 2014, www.brainyquote.com/quotes/authors/f/freddie_prinze.html.

4. G. Llewellyn and A. Silver, "Great Educational Quotes," The Learning Revolution Project, 2014, accessed November 8, 2014, http://learning revolution.com/page/great-educational-quotes.

5. John W. Gardner, "John W. Gardner Quotes," BrainyQuote, 2014, accessed January 19, 2014, www.brainyquote.com/quotes/quotes/j/johnw gard150841.html.

6. John Taylor Gatto, *Dumbing Us Down: The Hidden Curriculum of Compulsory Schooling* (Gabriola Island, BC: New Society Publishers, 2005), 21.

7. Stuart Patterson, "Headmaster Bans School Bell 'to Make Pupils Calmer,'" *Daily Record*, July 1, 2012, accessed July 20, 2015, www.dailyrecord.co.uk /news/scottish-news/headmaster-bans-school-bell-to-1071918#TBoITikhJHYy ACrK.97.

8. Anu Partanen, "What Americans Keep Ignoring about Finland's School Success," *Atlantic*, December 29, 2011, accessed July 25, 2014, www .theatlantic.com/national/archive/2011/12/what-americans-keep-ignoring-about-finlands-school-success/250564/.

9. John Holt, *How Children Fail* (New York: Perseus Group, 1982), 264.

10. Alan Bennett, "Alan Bennett Quotes," BrainyQuote, 2015, accessed October 15, 2015, www.brainyquote.com/quotes/authors/a/alan_bennett.html.

11. Albert Einstein, "Quotable Quote," Goodreads, 2016, accessed October 15, 2015, www.goodreads.com/quotes/19914-it-is-in-fact-nothing-short-of-a-miracle-that.

12. Amelia Thomson-Deveaux, "Should States Spend Billions to Reduce Class Sizes?" *FiveThirtyEight*, December 11, 2014, accessed July 10, 2015, http://fivethirtyeight.com/features/should-states-spend-billions-to-reduce-class-sizes/.

13. Ibid.

14. Ernest Istook, "Top Quotes of Ernest Istook," Quotehood, 2015, accessed July 19, 2015, www.quotehood.com/author/Ernest-Istook-quotes.

15. Alexander T. Tabarrok, "Tuning In to Dropping Out," The Independent Institute, March 4, 2012, accessed July 19, 2015, www.independent.org/ printer.asp?page=%2Fnewsroom%2Farticle.asp?id=3268.

16. Sufjan Stevens, cited in Lynsey Hanley, "State Trouper," *Guardian*, November 20, 2005, accessed July 19, 2015, www.theguardian.com/music/ 2005/nov/20/popandrock.sufjanstevens.

12. TEN "UN"COMMANDMENTS (PART 2)

1. Ken Robinson, "TED and Reddit Asked Sir Ken Robinson Anything—and He Answered," *TED Blog*, August 12, 2009, accessed July 20, 2015, http://blog.ted.com/tedandreddit1/.

2. Ken Robinson, "Fertile Minds Need Feeding," interview by J. Shepherd, *Guardian*, February 9, 2009, www.theguardian.com/education/2009/feb/10/teaching-sats.

3. Paul Black and Dylan Wiliam, "Inside the Black Box: Raising Standards through Classroom Assessment," *Phi Delta Kappan* 80, no. 2 (1998): 139–48, http://weaeducation.typepad.co.uk/files/blackbox-1.pdf.

4. V. Saxena, "Young Teacher Hands in Epic Letter Announcing Her Resignation . . . Now It's Going Viral," *Conservative Tribune*, October 31, 2015, accessed November 1, 2015, http://conservativetribune.com/young-teacher-epic-letter/?utmsource=Facebook&utmmedium=CTPages&utmcontent=2015-11-02&utmcampaign=manualpost.

5. Alfie Kohn, "Moving beyond Facts, Skills, and Right Answers," AlfieKohn.org, accessed July 21, 2015, www.alfiekohn.org/article/moving-beyond-facts-skills-right-answers/.

6. Ibid.

7. Ibid.

8. Eleanor Duckworth, "On the Virtues of Knowing the Virtues of Not Knowing," *Teach, Brain, Teach* (blog), March 18, 2011, accessed July 21, 2015, http://teachbrainteach.blogspot.com/2011/03/on-virtues-of-not.html.

9. Jonathan Nuckols, *Gaiam Life* (blog), 2015, accessed July 21, 2015, http://blog.gaiam.com/quotes/authors/jonathan-nuckols/60075.

10. Dave Ramsey, "Grades," BrainyQuote, 2015, accessed July 21, 2015, www.brainyquote.com/search_results.html?q=grades.

11. William Glasser, "William Glasser Quotes," BrainyQuote, 2015, accessed July 21, 2015, www.brainyquote.com/quotes/quotes/w/williamgla345806.html.

12. Anatole France, "Anatole France Quotes," BrainyQuote, 2015, accessed July 22, 2015, www.brainyquote.com/quotes/authors/a/anatole_france.html.

13. Ken Robinson, "How Schools Stifle Creativity," *TEDTalk Tuesdays*, CNN.com, November 3, 2009, accessed August 5, 2015, www.cnn.com/2009/OPINION/11/03/robinson.schools.stifle.creativity/index.html?iref=24hours.

14. Ivan Illich, *Deschooling Society* (London: Marion Boyers, 1971), 39.

15. Charlie Fink, "Charlie Fink Quotes," BrainyQuote, 2015, accessed August 5, 2015, www.brainyquote.com/quotes/authors/c/charlie_fink.html.

16. Lewis Thomas, "Lewis Thomas Quotes," BrainyQuote, 2015, accessed August 5, 2015, www.brainyquote.com/quotes/quotes/l/lewisthoma470030

.html.

17. Robinson, "How Schools Stifle Creativity."

18. Walter Annenberg, "Walter Annenberg Quotes," BrainyQuote, 2015, accessed August 5, 2015, www.brainyquote.com/quotes/quotes/w/walteranne322369.html.

19. Albert Einstein, "Quotable Quote," Goodreads, 2015, accessed August 5, 2015, www.goodreads.com/quotes/253933-i-never-teach-my-pupils-i-only-attempt-to-provide.

20. *Waiting for Superman*, directed by D. Guggenheim, October 29, 2010 (Hollywood, CA: Paramount Pictures, 2010).

21. Condoleezza Rice, "Condoleezza Rice Quotes," BrainyQuote, 2015, accessed August 5, 2015, www.brainyquote.com/quotes/quotes/c/condoleezz453867.html.

22. Hilary Swank, "Hilary Swank Quotes," BrainyQuote, 2015, accessed August 5, 2015, www.brainyquote.com/quotes/quotes/h/hilaryswan432453.html.

23. Kevin O'Leary, "Kevin O'Leary Quotes," BrainyQuote, 2015, accessed August 5, 2015, www.brainyquote.com/quotes/authors/k/kevin_oleary.html#txuPW6fCAgCxerj2.99.

13. THE RECOVERY PROCESS

1. Susan McLester, "Rick and Becky DuFour: Professional Communities at Work," *District Administration*, September 2012, accessed January 30, 2016, www.districtadministration.com/article/rick-and-becky-dufour.

2. Ken Robinson, *The Element: How Finding Your Passion Changes Everything* (New York: Penguin, 2009), 74.

3. Theodor Geisel (Dr. Seuss), *The Lorax* (New York: Random House, 1971).

BIBLIOGRAPHY

Allen, Ann Taylor. "American and German Women in the Kindergarten Movement, 1850–1914." In *German Influences on Education in the United States to 1917*, edited by Henry Geitz, Jürgen Heideking, and Jurgen Herbst, 85–102. Cambridge: Cambridge University Press, 2006. Accessed September 27, 2015. http://www.cambridge.org/us/academic/subjects/history/american-history-general-interest/german-influences-education-united-states-1917.

Annenberg, Walter. "Walter Annenberg Quotes." BrainyQuote, 2015. Accessed August 5, 2015. http://www.brainyquote.com/quotes/quotes/w/walteranne322369.html.

Barr, Jessica. "The Philosophy of Education." Froebel Web, 2006. Accessed September 15, 2015. http://www.froebelweb.org/web2005.html.

Bennett, Alan. "Alan Bennett Quotes." BrainyQuote, 2015. Accessed October 15, 2015. http://www.brainyquote.com/quotes/authors/a/alan_bennett.html.

Berg, Ellen. "Kindergarten." *Encyclopedia of Children and Childhood in History and Society*. Faqs.org, 2008. Accessed September 27, 2015. http://www.faqs.org/childhood/Ke-Me/Kindergarten.html.

Berry, Susan. "Berkeley Math Professor Ratner: Common Core 'Will Move U.S. Closer to Bottom in International Ranking.'" *Breitbart*, August 6, 2014. Accessed September 1, 2014. http://www.breitbart.com/big-government/2014/08/06/berkeley-math-professor-ratner-common-core-will-move-u-s-closer-to-bottom-in-international-ranking/.

———. "Education Expert Dr. Sandra Stotsky: Common Core 'Rather Shady.'" *Breitbart*, January 16, 2014. Accessed September 1, 2014. http://www.breitbart.com/big-government/2014/01/16/expert-dr-sandra-stotsky-on-common-core-we-are-a-very-naive-people/.

Black, Paul, and Dylan Wiliam. "Inside the Black Box: Raising Standards through Classroom Assessment." *Phi Delta Kappan* 80, no. 2 (1998): 139–48. http://weaeducation.typepad.co.uk/files/blackbox-1.pdf.

California Department of Education. "Common Core State Standards." California Department of Education, March 7, 2016. Accessed July 10, 2015. http://www.cde.ca.gov/re/cc/.

———. "Suspension and Expulsion Report." Data Quest, 2014. Accessed July 19, 2015. http://dq.cde.ca.gov/dataquest/SuspExp/umirsedcode.aspx?cYear=201314&cType=ALL&cCDS=00000000000000&cName=Statewide&cLevel=State&cChoic=UMIRS&ReportCode=UMIRS.

———. "Truancy Report." Data Quest, 2014. Accessed July 9, 2015. http://dq.cde.ca.gov/dataquest/SuspExp/TruancyReport.aspx?cYear=201314&cType=ALL&cCDS=00000000000000&cName=Statewide&cLevel=State&cChoic=TruRate&ReportCode=TruRate.

Douglas-Gabriel, Danielle. "The Controversial Idea That Could Lower Student Debt." *Washington Post Blog*, December 2, 2014. Accessed January 15, 2015. http://www.washingtonpost.com/blogs/wonkblog/wp/2014/12/02/why-so-many-students-are-spending-six-years-getting-a-college-degree/.

Duckworth, Eleanor. "On the Virtues of Knowing the Virtues of Not Knowing." *Teach, Brain, Teach* (blog), March 18, 2011. Accessed July 21, 2015. http://teachbrainteach.blogspot.com/2011/03/on-virtues-of-knowing-virtues-of-not.html.

Edison, Thomas Alva. "The Most Poignant Quotes." Famous Quotes, 2004. Accessed July 10, 2015. http://www.quotes.stevenredhead.com/ThomasEdison.html.

Einstein, Albert. "Albert Einstein Quotes for Enlightenment." True-Enlightenment, 2013. Accessed June 17, 2015. http://www.true-enlightenment.com/albert-einstein-quotes.html.

———. "Quotable Quote." Goodreads, 2015. Accessed August 5, 2015. http://www.goodreads.com/quotes/253933-i-never-teach-my-pupils-i-only-attempt-to-provide.

———. "Quotable Quote." Goodreads, 2016. Accessed October 15, 2015. http://www.goodreads.com/quotes/19914-it-is-in-fact-nothing-short-of-a-miracle-that.

Fink, Charlie. "Charlie Fink Quotes." BrainyQuote, 2015. Accessed August 5, 2015. http://www.brainyquote.com/quotes/authors/c/charlie_fink.html.

France, Anatole. "Anatole France Quotes." BrainyQuote, 2015. Accessed July 22, 2015. http://www.brainyquote.com/quotes/authors/a/anatole_france.html.

Gardner, John W. "John W. Gardner Quotes." BrainyQuote, 2014. Accessed January 19, 2014. http://www.brainyquote.com/quotes/quotes/j/johnwgard150841.html.

Gatto, John Taylor. *Dumbing Us Down: The Hidden Curriculum of Compulsory Schooling.* Gabriola Island, BC: New Society Publishers, 2005.

———. *Weapons of Mass Instruction: A School Teacher's Journey through the Dark World of Compulsory Education.* Gabriola Island, BC: New Society Publishers, 2010.

Geisel, Theodor (Dr. Seuss). *The Lorax.* New York: Random House, 1971.

Glasser, William. "William Glasser Quotes." BrainyQuote, 2015. Accessed July 21, 2015. http://www.brainyquote.com/quotes/quotes/w/williamgla345806.html.

Goyal, Nikhil. *One Size Does Not Fit All: A Student's Assessment of School.* New York: Alternative Education Resource Organization, 2012.

Hamblin, James. "Exercise Is ADHD Medication." *The Atlantic*, September 29, 2014. Accessed October 30, 2015. http://www.theatlantic.com/health/archive/2014/09/exercise-seems-to-be-beneficial-to-children/380844/?utm_content=buffer5e760&utm_medium=social&utm_source=facebook.com&utm_campaign=buffer.

Hanley, Lynsey. "State Trouper." *Guardian*, November 20, 2005. Accessed July 19, 2015. http://www.theguardian.com/music/2005/nov/20/popandrock.sufjanstevens.

Holmes, O. W. *Goodreads.* 2015. Accessed August 6, 2015. www.goodreads.com/quotes/37815-the-mind-once-stretched-by-a-new-idea-never-returns.

Holt, John. *How Children Fail.* New York: DeCapo Press, 1964. Reprint, New York: Perseus Group, 1982.

———. *Instead of Education: Ways to Help People Do Things Better.* Boulder, CO: Sentient Publications, 2004.

Illich, Ivan. *Deschooling Society.* London: Marion Boyers, 1971.

Istook, Ernest. "Top Quotes of Ernest Istook." Quotehood, 2015. Accessed July 19, 2015. http://www.quotehood.com/author/Ernest-Istook-quotes.

Kohn, Alfie. "Just Another Brick in the Wall: How Education Researchers Ignore the Ends to Tweak the Means." AlfieKohn.org, June 4, 2014. Accessed July 19, 2015. http://www.alfiekohn.org/blogs/brick/.

———. "Moving beyond Facts, Skills, and Right Answers." AlfieKohn.org. Accessed July 21, 2015. http://www.alfiekohn.org/article/moving-beyond-facts-skills-right-answers/. Originally published in "Getting Teaching and Learning Wrong," in *The Schools Our Children Deserve* by Alfie Kohn. Boston: Houghton Mifflin, 1999.

———. *Punished by Rewards: The Trouble with Gold Stars Incentive Plans, A's, Praise, and Other Bribes.* New York: Houghton Mifflin Harcourt, 1993.

Lindsey, Randall B., Laraine Roberts, and Franklin Campbell Jones. *The Culturally Proficient School: An Implementation Guide for School Leaders.* Thousand Oaks, CA: Corwin Press, 2005.

Llewellyn, G., and A. Silver. "Great Educational Quotes." The Learning Revolution Project, 2014. Accessed November 8, 2014. http://learningrevolution.com/page/great-educational-quotes.

Maryland State Board of Education. "Maryland Public Schools Suspension by School and Major Offense Category: In-School and Out-of-School Suspensions and Expulsions 2012–2013." Maryland State Board of Education, October 20, 2013. Accessed July 19, 2015. http://www.marylandpublicschools.org/MSDE/divisions/planningresultstest/doc/20122013Student/susp13_sch_comb.pdf.

McLester, Susan. "Rick and Becky DuFour: Professional Communities at Work." *District Administration,* September 2012. Accessed January 30, 2016. http://www.districtadministration.com/article/rick-and-becky-dufour.

Merriam-Webster Dictionary. "Rigor." *Merriam-Webster Dictionary,* 2015. Accessed August 19, 2015. http://www.merriam-webster.com/dictionary/rigor.

———. "Rigor Mortis." *Merriam-Webster Dictionary,* 2015. Accessed August 19, 2015. http://www.merriam-webster.com/dictionary/rigor%20mortis.

Mintz, Jerry. "The Ten Signs You Need to Find a Different Education for Your Child." Alternative Education Resource Organization, October 12, 2015. Accessed November 15, 2015. http://www.educationrevolution.org/store/thetensigns/.

Nielson, Lisa. "I Am No Longer Willing to Hurt Children—John Taylor Gatto (A Compilation)." *The Innovative Educator* (blog), January 18, 2011. Accessed October 11, 2014. http://theinnovativeeducator.blogspot.com/2011/01/i-am-no-longer-willing-to-hurt-children.html.

Nuckols, Jonathan. *Gaiam Life* (blog), 2015. Accessed July 21, 2015. http://blog.gaiam.com/quotes/authors/jonathan-nuckols/60075.

O'Leary, Kevin. "Kevin O'Leary Quotes." BrainyQuote, 2015. Accessed August 5, 2015. http://www.brainyquote.com/quotes/authors/k/kevin_oleary.html#txuPW6fCAgCxerj2.99.

Partanen, Anu. "What Americans Keep Ignoring about Finland's School Success." *Atlantic,* December 29, 2011. Accessed July 25, 2014. http://www.theatlantic.com/national/archive/2011/12/what-americans-keep-ignoring-about-finlands-school-success/250564/.

Patterson, Stuart. "Headmaster Bans School Bell 'to Make Pupils Calmer.'" *Daily Record,* July 1, 2012. Accessed July 20, 2015. http://www.dailyrecord.co.uk/news/scottish-news/headmaster-bans-school-bell-to-1071918#TBoITikhJHYyACrK.97.

Planty, Michael, William Hussar, and Thomas Snyder (National Center for Education Statistics), and Grace Kena, Angelina Kewal-Ramani, Jana Kemp, Kevin Bianco, and Rachel Dinkes (American Institutes for Research). "The Condition of Education 2009." National Center for Education Statistics, May 28, 2009. Accessed September 29, 2013. https://nces.ed.gov/pubsearch/pubsinfo.asp?pubid=2009081.

Prinze, Freddie. "Freddie Prinze Quotes." BrainyQuote, 2014. Accessed August 8, 2014. http://www.brainyquote.com/quotes/authors/f/freddie_prinze.html.

Ramsey, Dave. "Grades." BrainyQuote, 2015. Accessed July 21, 2015. http://www.brainyquote.com/search_results.html?q=grades.

Ravitch, Diane. Interview by *School of Thought.* PBS, 2016. Accessed September 1, 2014. http://www.thirteen.org/eye-on-education/diane-ravitch/#.UTt6Cdacdrg.

Rice, Condoleezza. "Condoleezza Rice Quotes." BrainyQuote, 2015. Accessed August 5, 2015. http://www.brainyquote.com/quotes/quotes/c/condoleezz453867.html.

Robinson, Ken. "Do Schools Kill Creativity?" TED, June 2006. Accessed August 5, 2015. https://www.ted.com/talks/ken_robinson_says_schools_kill_creativity/transcript?language=en.

———. *The Element: How Finding Your Passion Changes Everything.* New York: Penguin, 2009.

———. "Fertile Minds Need Feeding." Interview by J. Shepherd. *Guardian,* February 9, 2009. http://www.theguardian.com/education/2009/feb/10/teaching-sats.

———. "How Schools Kill Creativity." Computer Users in Education, 2007. Monterey Technology Conference.

———. "How Schools Stifle Creativity." *TEDTalk Tuesdays*. CNN.com, November 3, 2009. Accessed August 5, 2015. http://www.cnn.com/2009/OPINION/11/03/robinson.schools .stifle.creativity/index.html?iref=24hours.

———. *Out of Our Minds: Learning to Be Creative*. West Sussex: Capstone Publishing, 2011.

———. "TED and Reddit Asked Sir Ken Robinson Anything—and He Answered." *TED Blog*, August 12, 2009. Accessed July 20, 2015. http://blog.ted.com/ted_and_reddit_1/.

———. "Three Principles That Our Education Systems Are Based." Twitter, June 21, 2015. https://twitter.com/ukedchat/status/612583280500678656.

Rothbard, M. N. "Mises Institute Austrian Economics, Freedom, and Peace." *Mises Daily*, September 9, 2006. Accessed July 2, 2015. https://mises.org/library/education-free-and-compulsory-0.

Samuels, Christina. "Just 15 States Require Students to Attend Kindergarten." *Education Week*, September 19, 2014. Accessed August 7, 2015. http://www.huffingtonpost.com/2014/09/19/kindergarten-laws_n_5851724.html.

Saxena, V. "Young Teacher Hands in Epic Letter Announcing Her Resignation . . . Now It's Going Viral." *Conservative Tribune*, October 31, 2015. Accessed November 1, 2015. http://conservativetribune.com/young-teacher-epic-letter/?utm_source=Facebook&utm _medium=CTPages&utm_content=2015-11-02&utm_campaign=manualpost.

Sheehy, Kelsey. "Homeschooled Students Well-Prepared for College, Study Finds." *Huffington Post*, June 1, 2012. Accessed September 2, 2014. http://www.huffingtonpost.com/2012/06/01/homeschooled-studentswel_n_1562425.html.

Swank, Hilary. "Hilary Swank Quotes." BrainyQuote, 2015. Accessed August 5, 2015. http://www.brainyquote.com/quotes/quotes/h/hilaryswan432453.html.

Tabarrok, Alexander T. "Tuning In to Dropping Out." The Independent Institute, March 4, 2012. Accessed July 19, 2015. http://www.independent.org/printer.asp?page =%2Fnewsroom%2Farticle.asp?id=3268.

Thomas, Lewis. "Lewis Thomas Quotes." BrainyQuote, 2015. Accessed August 5, 2015. http://www.brainyquote.com/quotes/quotes/l/lewisthoma470030.html.

Thomson-Deveaux, Amelia. "Should States Spend Billions to Reduce Class Sizes?" *FiveThirtyEight*, December 11, 2014. Accessed July 10, 2015. http://fivethirtyeight.com/features/should-states-spend-billions-to-reduce-class-sizes/.

United States Department of Education. "Four Ways to Stay Connected to Our 2015 Back to School Bus Tour." *Homeroom* (blog). Accessed August 30, 2015. http://blog.ed.gov/2015/09/four-ways-to-stay-connected-with-our-2015-back-to-school-bus-tour/.

———. "Institute of Educational Sciences IES." National Center for Education Statistics, March 2015. Accessed September 29, 2015. http://nces.ed.gov/fastfacts/display .asp?id=372.

Waiting for Superman. Directed by D. Guggenheim, October 29, 2010. Hollywood, CA: Paramount Pictures, 2010.

ABOUT THE AUTHOR

Evonne Espey Rogers has served as an educator in Pennsylvania, Maryland, and California. She has been a classroom teacher, a school and central office administrator, and a county coordinator and director; she ended her schooling career as a district assistant superintendent.

Having spent her entire life in and around schools, she cares deeply about teaching and learning. Her experiences in schools have led her to speak and write, with passion, about what she has observed over the years. Her belief is that all children deserve to have conditions in which they can thrive, grow, and learn without fear of threat, intimidation, failure, or coercion. Her desire is that schools become true partners in facilitating the unique and individualized education every young person deserves.

Made in the USA
San Bernardino, CA
13 June 2019